Studies in Sociology

Edited by
PROFESSOR W. M. WILLIAMS
University College, Swansea

7
THE STRUCTURE OF SOCIAL SCIENCE

STUDIES IN SOCIOLOGY
Edited by Professor W. M. Williams

THE STRUCTURE OF SOCIAL SCIENCE

A Philosophical Introduction

Michael H. Lessnoff
Lecturer in Politics, University of Glasgow

LONDON · GEORGE ALLEN & UNWIN LTD
RUSKIN HOUSE   MUSEUM STREET

First published in 1974

© *George Allen & Unwin Ltd. 1974*

ISBN 0 04 300045 2 hardback
0 04 300046 0 paperback

Printed in Great Britain
in 10 point Plantin type
by Unwin Brothers Limited
The Gresham Press
Old Woking, Surrey

INTRODUCTION AND ACKNOWLEDGMENTS

In this book I try to deal in short compass with a large subject – the philosophy of social science. I have tried to avoid superficiality, and yet at the same time to discuss a range of issues broad enough to constitute a tolerably general introduction to the subject. Inevitably, an introductory book in philosophy is a survey of controversies. My aim has been, always, to state as clearly and to argue as persuasively as possible my own view, while at the same time putting fully before the reader opposing views and arguments. I am, however, only too well aware that many relevant issues have not been raised, and that a good deal has been taken for granted that might be challenged. This, I believe, is inevitable – in philosophy some things have to be taken for granted in order that other things can be discussed. However, the reader is entitled to a special word of explanation in relation to the first chapter, which deals with the philosophy of physical science. I have chosen to develop my theme by comparing (and contrasting) the social sciences with the physical sciences; hence I begin by setting out what I take the relevant elements of the philosophy of physical science to be. Here, though, the exposition has had to be somewhat dogmatic. There simply was no space (nor would it have been appropriate) to argue through all the controversies in the field; hence I have contented myself with expounding a more-or-less 'positivist' account – an account which I believe would (in broad outline) be rather widely accepted, and which I believe I *could* defend in more detail than I have been able to do in this book.

In the pages of this book, I frequently discuss arguments put forward by particular individuals. Nevertheless, the book is not concerned with individuals as such, but with ideas. I have not been concerned to give a 'balanced' or comprehensive account of the views or work of these individuals as a whole; rather, I have used the arguments they put forward in particular places to illustrate various themes. This does not, of course, mean that I have felt free to misrepresent individuals – on the contrary, I have striven very hard to avoid doing so; that is, to expound correctly the arguments I discuss. But I have not (indeed, could not possibly have) attempted to follow all the nuances and even inconsistencies of an individual's views throughout his entire life's work.

There is one feature of this book that is perhaps a little unusual in a book on the philosophy of social science; namely, the amount of space devoted to a few elementary aspects of statistical method. This section may perhaps be found difficult by some, but I would ask them to persevere. Correlation and significance tests play such a large role in the practice of social science that it seemed to me essential to bring a philosophical perspective to bear on the procedures involved – something which, in my view, is all too rarely done.

As is the case with all authors, I have received much help from many people in the writing of this book. I am particularly grateful to Mary Haight, Jim Edwards, Nick Bunnin, and Steven Lukes, who read through the entire text. In addition, individual chapters and sections were read by Gerald Lessnoff, Professor S. D. Silvey, Peter Norman, Professor T. D. Campbell, Terry Greenwood, Scott Meikle, Diane Dawson and Alastair Weir. I benefited, also, from discussions with Professor A. M. Potter, Keith Burton, and Nick Fisher. From all of them I received valuable suggestions, and their advice has enabled me to correct a number of errors; for those that remain, I (like all who write acknowledgments) accept full responsibility. To Professor David Raphael, who was my first teacher in philosophy and first turned my mind towards the philosophy of social science, I owe an inestimable debt of gratitude. My grateful thanks are also due to Charlotte Logan, Sheila Hamilton and Jean Beverly, who miraculously transformed my illegible handwriting into a neat typescript.

Chapter 5 of this book is partly based on an earlier article of mine, 'Functionalism and Explanation in Social Science', which appeared in the *Sociological Review*, new series, vol. 17 (1969).

Michael Lessnoff
Glasgow

September 1973

CONTENTS

TO MY PARENTS

NOTE ON FOOTNOTES

Full references are given only on the first occasion that a particular title is referred to; thereafter abbreviated references only are given. The full references can be traced by using the Name Index.

CHAPTER 1

Physical Science

IT may seem surprising to begin a book on the philosophy of social science with a chapter on physical science, but there is good reason to do so. The physical sciences (especially physics itself) have a long tradition behind them, and a record of brilliant intellectual achievement. As a result, they pervade our conception of 'science' as such. Their characteristics tend to be taken as standards that any discipline which aspires to that honorific title must attain. By contrast, the achievements of the social sciences seem, with some exceptions, rather meagre. This gives rise to the following state of affairs. On the one hand, there is a powerful aspiration for a body of 'scientific' knowledge of social life, comparable in quantity and quality to our scientific knowledge of physical nature. On the other, there also exist strong doubts as to whether social life is in fact a subject-matter suited to the physical science model. Many issues in the philosophy of social science centre on disputes between these two schools of thought, disputes as to whether particular features of the physical sciences are, or can be, or should be, also features of a systematic study of social life. Clearly, then, it is necessary to pay some attention to the salient features of physical science.

Laws of Nature
According to the physical science model, the primary aim of science is to discover and state the Laws of Nature. A familiar example of such a law is Newton's Law of Gravitation, expressed by the formula

$$F = G. \frac{m_1 \times m_2}{r^2}$$

(or, in words: Every particle of matter attracts every other particle of matter with a force (F) proportional to the product of their masses (m) divided by the square of the distance (r) between them). This example illustrates some of the general characteristics of Laws of Nature, which must now be made explicit. (The initial discussion below deliberately ignores a number of complications and controversies. Some of these are taken up later.)

First, a Law of Nature is a statement that purports to describe *how the world is*. It is not a *prescriptive or evaluative* statement – that is, it does not prescribe how the world ought to be, nor evaluate the goodness or badness of any state of the world actual or conceivable. Equally, it is not an *analytic* statement. A statement is analytic if its truth is guaranteed by the meaning of the words it contains, for example, 'All men are male'. Given that 'men' means 'male persons', this statement is equivalent to a tautology. To deny an analytic or tautological statement is to contradict oneself; to deny a Law of Nature involves no self-contradiction, for even if the Law is true the world might have been other than it is. Pure mathematics is analytic – its truth is logically entailed by the definition of its terms – and so is not a science in the present sense.

A statement asserting how the world is may be true or false. Some method, therefore, is required for appraising such an assertion, involving a criterion of justification. Science has a characteristic method and criterion for justifying its laws, that is, by comparing what they assert about the world with *systematic observation of the world as it appears to the senses* – the so-called empirical method. Thus, observations of bodies and their motions provided the justification for accepting Newton's Law of Gravitation as a Law of Nature. This empirical basis of scientific laws distinguishes them from other sorts of statements purporting to describe how the world is, such as are found in theology and some branches of philosophy. These statements are not amenable to empirical justification because of the sort of entities to which they refer – such as deities, angels, devils, the Forms of Plato, or the Absolute of Hegel.

Next, a Law of Nature is a statement of *unrestrictedly universal* form. It asserts something about *all* instances of a class of phenomena, and the class is defined without any restriction of time or place. The Law of Gravitation makes an assertion about all material particles, in whatever part of the universe, at all times, past, present, and future. The universal form of Laws of Nature can be represented by the following formulae:

'*All* As are B.'
'*Whenever* A is the case, B is the case.'

The Law of Gravitation can be put into these forms as follows:

'All material particles [As] are attracted by all other material particles with a force . . . [B]'

'Whenever material particles exist [A], every particle attracts every other particle with a force . . . [B]'

Laws of Nature vary in their *generality*. The Law of Gravitation is an extremely general law, that is, it applies to a very wide range of entities – in fact, to every body in the universe. In principle, a universal statement such as a Law of Nature may apply to arbitrarily few entities, and even to no entities at all; but the more general a scientific law is, the more it is prized as 'fundamental' (and if a universal empirical statement has very little generality, one would scarcely call it a Law of Nature). A Law of Nature rather less general than the Law of Gravitation is Archimedes' Principle:

A body wholly or partly immersed in a fluid loses weight by an amount equal to the weight of the fluid it displaces.

This Law is unrestrictedly universal, since it applies to *all* immersed bodies at all times and places; but it is less general than the Law of Gravitation, since it applies only to *immersed* bodies.

By virtue of their universality, Laws of Nature permit the deduction of *hypothetical predictions*. Thus, Archimedes' Principle yields the hypothetical prediction that, if a given object (x) is immersed in a fluid, its weight will be reduced by the weight of fluid it displaces. The deduction proceeds similarly to Aristotle's syllogism:

Major premise: All bodies immersed in fluid lose weight . . .

Minor premise: x is a body

Conclusion: If x is immersed in fluid it will lose weight. . . .

It is tautological that, if the premises of a deduction are true, the conclusion is true. In the present case, it is tautologically true that, if all bodies immersed in fluid lose weight and x is a body, then if x is immersed in fluid it will lose weight. That Laws of Nature, if true, yield true predictions as to what will be the case in certain conditions, is of course the source of their practical usefulness.

Laws of Nature are not all of the same kind. Let us here note two kinds, causal laws and laws of functional dependence.[1] A *causal law* states a relation of regular succession between *events* (i.e. changes of state) of specified types, for example, 'When an object is heated, it expands'. Alternatively, one might say: 'Heating an object *causes* it to

[1] These (and other) types of laws are distinguished in E. Nagel, *The Structure of Science* (London, Routledge and Kegan Paul, 1961), pp. 75–8.

expand'. *Laws of functional dependence* state constant relations in the magnitude of variables – an example is Newton's Law of Gravitation, which refers, not to successive events, but to the relation between the masses of bodies, their distance apart, and the force of attraction between them. From it, however, many causal laws can be derived: 'When two bodies move apart, the gravitational attraction between them decreases'; 'When a body loses mass, the gravitational attraction it exerts on other bodies decreases'; and so on. A law of functional dependence is often a sort of envelope that includes a large number of causal laws, and thus a more economical, and hence preferable, way of stating them.

An important way in which Laws of Nature vary is in *precision*. A first distinction here is between qualitative and quantitative laws. A *qualitative* law asserts a relation between things and/or their qualities without specifying any numerical values (e.g. 'When a spark is passed through a mixture of hydrogen and oxgyen gas, water is formed'). As for *quantitative* laws, they specify the relation between magnitudes, either roughly (e.g. 'The hotter a body becomes the more it expands') or exactly. Newton's Law of Gravitation and Archimedes' Principle are exact quantitative laws – the former tells us, not only that all bodies attract one another (a qualitative law), or that the nearer and more massive bodies are the more they attract each other (a rough quantitative law), but the exact numerical relation between mass, distance, and attractive force. The more precise a scientific law, the more highly it is prized; hence the tendency to formulate exact quantitative laws whenever possible. But precision is not the only virtue of laws; generality, as we saw above, is another. Some laws, such as Newton's Law of Gravitation, combine great generality and great precision, but sometimes the two desiderata conflict. Thus a relatively imprecise law like 'When an object is heated, it expands' is valuable because it is more general than any of the more precise laws dealing with heating and expansion (the exact quantitative relation between these phenomena is given for each substance by its coefficient of expansion).

The problem of induction
It is now time to confront a notorious and fundamental problem concerning the idea of Laws of Nature – namely, that we have no adequate grounds for believing that any Law of Nature is true. A Law of Nature is an unrestrictedly universal empirical statement. To see the problem this gives rise to, consider the trivial (but much-quoted) 'law', 'All crows are black', and the singular empirical statement 'x is a black crow'. The latter, as an empirical statement, is to be justified by observation of x – by a person who knows what a crow looks like and has normal colour vision, etc. This is relatively unproblematic because x

occupies a limited region of space and time. But an unrestrictedly universal statement refers, potentially, to *all* space and time. 'All crows are black' is equivalent to 'In every place in the universe, and at every time (past, present, or future) if there is a crow, it is black'. To justify such a statement by observation, in the same sense as the singular statement 'x is a black crow' can be justified by observation, it would be necessary to observe every place in the universe at every moment of time in order to discover if there was then a crow there, and if so whether it was black. Clearly, this is impossible and even, in so far as it refers to the future, nonsensical. The statement 'All crows *so far observed* are black' can be empirically justified, but logic cannot bridge the gulf between this and the law 'All crows are black', however many crows have been observed. To reason from a report of observations to an unrestricted law – that is, *inductively* – is to risk error, as experience indeed confirms. Further observation always may, and frequently does, contradict a law until then abundantly supported by empirical evidence. Such indeed has been the fate of the laws of Newtonian mechanics, for centuries the very foundation of science.

Is there then any way to justify scientific laws ? Some attempts to do so are essentially arguments for the validity, in some sense, of inductive inference (that is, inference from statements of particular facts to unrestrictedly universal statements). One such argument, while admitting that the truth of a law is never *guaranteed* by any degree of inductive support, nevertheless asserts that strong inductive support can make it *probable*: that is, it is probable that the law 'All As are B' is true, if a sufficiently large number of As have been observed in a variety of circumstances, and all observed As were B (the larger the number of As observed, the greater the probability).

The acceptability of this argument turns on the meaning of an assertion that some statement is 'probably' true, which is far from clear. One reasonably clear-cut interpretation, however, is in terms of *relative frequency* (or proportion). Suppose we know that a bag contains 100 balls, of which 90 are black, and that one ball is to be picked out of the bag, there being no known reason to expect one ball rather than another to be picked; we may then say that the probability (chance) of

a black ball being picked, *relative to our knowledge*, is 9 out of 10 (or $\frac{9}{10}$).

This justifies saying that the statement 'The ball picked out will be black' is *probably true*. So would any proportion of black balls appreciably over half, and perhaps even barely over half.

Can we apply this argument to Laws of Nature ? Unfortunately not.[2]

---

[2] The reasoning here is based on K. R. Popper, *The Logic of Scientific Discovery*, revised edn (London, Hutchinson, 1968), p. 259.

In the case of the balls, we know (by hypothesis) that the statement 'This ball is black' is true for the majority of the balls in the bag. Correspondingly, to warrant the assertion that an unrestrictedly universal empirical statement which has strong inductive support is probably true, it must be *known* that the majority of such statements *are true*. But this cannot be the case; we have seen that no unrestrictedly universal empirical statement can be known to be true. And because of this, we now see, no such statement can be said to be probably true either, in the relative frequency sense of probability.

In fact, the idea that induction can justify the assertion that a Law of Nature is probably true compounds the difficulty it was meant to solve, for it requires that a *majority* of Laws having strong inductive support be true. To know this requires knowledge of the total number of such laws, including those not yet formulated, but which will be formulated in the future.

This impasse has led some writers to seek a solution through a different sense of probability, so-called *inductive probability*. According to P. F. Strawson,[3] it is analytic (i.e. true by definition) that the strength of the evidence for a law is in proportion to the number and variety of known favourable instances – in other words that the probability that it is true depends on the strength of its inductive support. If so, we appear to have a second sense of probability besides the relative frequency sense: namely, inductive probability. In fact, this notion need not rest on a definitional *fiat*, but may be justified in the following way. There is, we can suppose, a finite, though unknown, number of As in the universe (the universe itself being, apparently, finite in space and time). *A priori*, any A may or may not be B; thus, we can say that the probability that any A is B lies between 0 and 1 (i.e. between impossibility and certainty). Let us call this otherwise unknown probability p. Then, the probability that *all* As are B is p^n where n is the number of unobserved As (and, at first, the total number of As) in the universe. Now, every time an A is observed to be B (so long as no A is observed to be not-B), n declines and the probability that all As are B increases. However, this argument does not solve our problem. For it gives no grounds for supposing that any strength of inductive support actually makes the truth of a law *probable* (that is, more probable than not) – since n and p are unknown, no even moderately precise relationship is suggested between the probability of a law's truth and its inductive support, only that they increase and decrease together. At any moment, therefore, the probability that such a law is true may be indefinitely small. In fact, it seems very unlikely that any degree of inductive support could make the truth of a law

[3] See his 'Dissolving the Problem of Induction' in B. A. Broay (ed.), *Readings in the Philosophy of Science* (Englewood Cliffs, Prentice-Hall, 1970), pp. 590–6.

probable, since innumerable laws once held to be firmly established by abundant inductive evidence are now held to be, on the basis of further evidence, strictly false.

Yet there would appear to be a very strange paradox in the conclusion that the truth of universal laws cannot be even probable, for it seems to make all rational behaviour impossible. Rational behaviour depends on the predictability of future facts, which in turn seems to depend on the reliability of laws. If one wishes to avoid drowning one should avoid lengthy immersion in water – one should, in other words, act on the assumption that men always drown if immersed in water for long. It appears, in fact, to be rational and indeed inevitable constantly to act as if a huge number of inductively inferred laws are true. Hence, it could be argued, there *must* be good reason to believe that their truth is at least probable.

However, this is not so. What is required to enable us to act rationally is that, in *particular future cases*, there should be specifiable probable outcomes (we act always in particular cases, not universally). This too requires inductive inference, of a slightly different kind. We need to be able to say that, if all observed As are B, and the number of observed As is large, then any as yet unobserved A is probably B. This would explain why, if one wishes not to be drowned, it is rational to avoid lengthy immersion in water – for if on any particular occasion one does not, one will probably drown. Unfortunately, this inference cannot be justified if probability is understood in the relative frequency sense: for then, that an as yet unobserved A is probably B would imply that a majority of As so far unobserved are B, and this cannot be known, no matter how many observed As are B.

It seems, then, that in order to salvage the idea of rational behaviour we are forced to admit a different sense of probability, a special inductive sense relating to particular cases, such that, to assert that an as yet unobserved A is probably B implies that very many already observed As are B. That assertion, however, is quite independent of any assertion that the law 'All As are B' is probably true. Suppose that it is probable, but not certain, that an as yet unobserved A will be B, i.e. $\frac{1}{2} < p < 1$ (p is the probability in question). Then the probability that *all* as yet unobserved As will be B is p^n (where n is the number of as yet unobserved As). The size of p^n depends partly on n, which is unknown; if n is high, then no matter how high p is (so long as p is less than 1), p^n can be under a half and even very small indeed. But the probability that all As are B cannot exceed the probability that all unobserved As are B. So the probability that all As are B can be extremely small, no matter how great the probability that a particular unobserved A will be B. Indeed, even if it is certain that 'All As are B' is false (because one A is known to be not-B), it may still be very probable that a particular unobserved A is B, if a sufficiently large number of observed As were B. A single exception should not greatly affect the inductive probability relating to the particular unobserved case. The possibility of rational action does not, then, imply that Laws of Nature are probably true, much less that they are true.

Falsifiability

What, then, *is* the status of a scientific law? The most satisfactory answer to this question, that of Karl Popper,[4] is that it is a hypothesis that can never be definitely accepted – only provisionally, because no matter how strong the observational evidence in its favour, new evidence can always contradict it. Indeed, it is precisely this *empirical falsifiability* – that it can be contradicted by observed facts – that, for Popper, is the criterion of a scientific statement. When observed facts are in accord with a law, they are said by Popper to *corroborate* the law. So long as a law continues to be corroborated, it may be true; as soon as it is contradicted by observed facts, it must be false. The task of science is to subject laws to ever more and more various empirical tests, to discover to what extent the laws are corroborated and to what extent falsified.

In principle, the falsification of a law by a contrary instance is a clear-cut matter ('All As are B' is falsified by a single A which is not-B). But in practice it is more complex. A law rarely yields predictions that are empirically testable unless one makes further theoretical assumptions (called *auxiliary hypotheses*). Hence, if such a prediction is false, one can strictly deduce only that *either* the law or one or more of the auxiliary hypotheses (or both) must be false. Thus, an apparently falsified law can sometimes be 'rescued' by replacing one of the auxiliary hypotheses involved by a better one – indeed, it is quite normal for major new laws to win acceptance in this way, Newton's Law of Gravitation being a notable case in point.[5] According to Richard Feynman, Newton's Law is in conflict with observed motions of the satellites of Jupiter, on the assumption (widely held in the seventeenth century) that light is transmitted instantaneously. However, on the alternative (and now accepted) hypothesis that light takes time to travel through space, the discrepancy disappears.[6] Also – and

---

[4] See his *The Logic of Scientific Discovery*.

[5] See I. Lakatos, 'Falsification and the Methodology of Scientific Research Programmes', in I. Lakatos and A. Musgrave (eds), *Criticism and the Growth of Knowledge* (Cambridge U.P., 1970), esp. p. 133.

[6] R. Feynman, *The Character of Physical Law* (London, B.B.C., 1965), pp. 22–3. Feynman seems to be wrong, however, in asserting that the observations of Jupiter's satellites were designed as tests of Newton's Law, and that the Law thus led to the finite velocity theory of light. These observations led to the classic enunciation of the finite velocity theory (though not its universal accept-

very important – the theory that light has a finite velocity yields further empirically testable predictions different from those of its rival; and relevant observations corroborated the finite velocity theory.

This example also casts light on the criteria for accepting and rejecting scientific laws. The finite velocity theory of light transmission was preferred to its rival because it was (and is) more highly corroborated: that is, every observed fact that corroborates the other also corroborates the finite velocity theory, and the latter is also corroborated by observations that contradict the other. Such a relation between rival theories is of course always relative to a given body of evidence, and may always be altered by further evidence. But the rule for provisional acceptance of hypothetical Laws of Nature is: prefer any law that is more highly corroborated by the existing evidence than any rival. If a law has this status it should not be discarded as soon as it is falsified; it stands until replaced by a superior one. Thus Newton's Law of Gravitation held the field for many years, despite its disagreement with the observed motions of Mercury, because it was the best law available until it was superseded by Einstein's General Theory of Relativity. The position of quantum theory today is similar. Such a situation is, of course, a stimulus to seek a better theory.

The status of a law as better corroborated by the evidence than any rival holds, of course, only given accepted auxiliary hypotheses. These auxiliary hypotheses are accepted because they, in turn, are preferable to any rival, given further auxiliary hypotheses; and so on. The corpus of acceptable scientific laws is an interdependent system in which individual laws depend on one another in an infinite regress. But as Popper points out,[7] this regress is not vicious, for what depends on it is not truth but only a provisional acceptability always subject to revision in the light of further evidence.

Statistical laws

So far, for expository purposes, I have treated scientific laws as unrestrictedly universal empirical statements. In fact, however, some of the most fundamental laws of modern physics are not universal but statistical in form: they have the form, not 'All As are B' but 'x% of all As are B'. For example, by the wave equations of quantum mechanics it is possible, given the energy level of an atom, to calculate – not its diameter, for that is ruled out as a consequence of Heisenberg's Uncertainty Principle – but only the *probability* that it has a given diameter, or in other words, the *proportion* of atoms of a given energy

ance) in 1676; Newton's Law of Gravitation did not become known until the 1680s.

[7] *The Logic of Scientific Discovery*, pp. 104–5.

level that have a given diameter.[8] The laws governing atomic diameters are irreducibly statistical in form: 'x% of all atoms of a given energy level have a given diameter'.

It is obvious that such laws pose a problem for Popper's account of science in terms of the falsifiability of laws. Unrestricted statistical laws are in fact unfalsifiable in principle. To know that such a law is false (or true) would be to have knowledge of all the entities to which it refers, in all places and at all times, past, present and future. Only thus could one compare the proportion of these entities asserted by the law to have a given characteristic, with the proportion that actually has it. To put it another way; whatever the proportion of these entities observed to have the specified characteristic, the observed facts are consistent with the law, and in this sense corroborate it. The problem, then, is to find a way of limiting the range of data held to corroborate a statistical law.

One way out of the problem is via statistical sampling theory.[9] Suppose we wish to test the hypothesis 'x% of all As are B'. If the hypothesis is true, then in *large samples* of As, the proportion of As that are B will in the great majority of cases be very close to x%; that is, the probability that in a large sample of As the proportion of As that are B will be very close to x%, is very high. Suppose, now, we observe a large sample of As, and find that the proportion that are B differs from x% by a small amount, $\Delta x\%$. We cannot regard the hypothesis as falsified, for if it happens to be true, there is still a chance that a large sample will have a proportion of As that are B differing from x% by as much as $\Delta x\%$. How great a chance (or probability) depends on the size of Δx and of the sample (n): the larger n is, the smaller the probability for a given value of Δx; and the larger Δx, the smaller the probability for a given n.

Let us now make use of the idea, not of falsification, but of *discorroboration*. Let us say that a statistical hypothesis 'x% of all As are B' is discorroborated by an observed sample of As if the proportion of As that are B in the sample is one that would be 'very unlikely' to be observed if the hypothesis were true; that is, the hypothesis is discorroborated if Δx is sufficiently large. The next question, of course, is what value of Δx should be considered just large enough to discorroborate the hypothesis, given the size of the sample (n).

We know that, if the hypothesis is true, then for any given n, the probability of observing various values of Δx decreases as Δx increases. For each value of Δx there is thus an associated probability (or improbability) of its being observed if the hypothesis is true. But if n

[8] Cf. E. Nagel, *op. cit.*, p. 307.
[9] The account here departs somewhat from that of Popper in *The Logic of Scientific Discovery*, pp. 189–205. I owe to Mr J. S. Edwards the realization that such a departure is necessary.

is made sufficiently large, it is possible to specify a value of Δx which is in effect the same regardless of this associated probability (or improbability). (More precisely, the range of variation of Δx becomes negligibly small as this probability varies.) What is more, the larger the sample size, the more nearly does this value of Δx become completely insensitive to changes in the associated probability, and the smaller this value of Δx becomes. If n is sufficiently large (that is, very large indeed), this value of Δx becomes so small that *any* deviation from x% in the proportion of n As found to be B, can reasonably be taken as *discorroborating* the hypothesis that x% of all As are B. Correspondingly, if n is sufficiently large, we can say that a sample of n As *corroborates* the hypothesis that x% of all As are B only if x% of the sample of As are B.

Now, the statistical laws of quantum mechanics refer to very small-scale phenomena (individual atoms, fundamental particles, etc.): from them can be deduced predictions of the properties of large-scale phenomena which correspond to exceedingly large numbers of the small-scale ones. Observation of the large-scale phenomena is thus observation of very large samples of the small-scale ones; hence such observations afford a means of corroborating and discorroborating the laws in the sense explained. In this way, the quantum laws can be tested by empirical evidence, even though they can be neither verified nor falsified by it.

Explanation

The aim of science, we can say, is (in summary) to frame Laws of Nature that are as highly corroborated as possible by empirical evidence. Another way to put this, is that known facts should be *explicable* by the laws of science. To explain a fact is to show *why* it is as it is, to account for its being one thing rather than the innumerable other things it might conceivably have been. How is this done?

According to Carl Hempel's widely accepted account,[10] scientific explanation is, ideally, *deductive-nomological* in form, that is, it deduces the explanandum (the fact to be explained) from a set of premises which includes a Law of Nature. For example, suppose that the temperature is below zero (Centigrade), and there is snow on the ground; then the temperature rises above zero, and the snow melts. Why did the snow melt? The obvious explanation is, of course, that it melted *because* the temperature rose above zero. This explanation implies (though it does not state) that there is a *connection* between rising temperature and melting snow; to be precise, a Law of Nature

[10] See C. G. Hempel, *Philosophy of Natural Science* (Englewood Cliffs, Prentice-Hall, 1966), pp. 47–54.

that whenever the temperature of snow rises above zero, it melts. The explanation can be put in a form similar to the Aristotelian syllogism:

Major premise: Whenever the temperature of snow rises above 0°C, it melts.

Minor premise: The temperature of the snow rose above 0°C.

Conclusion: The snow melted. (Explanandum).

The explanandum is here deduced from two premises, a Law of Nature and a statement of a singular fact. The latter is the *cause* of the explanandum, and the major premise is thus a causal law. Given the premises, the conclusion follows necessarily; so that the premises (if true) show why the explanandum could not have been other than it was. By virtue of the law that forms the major premise, the cause stated in the minor premise is a *sufficient condition* of the occurrence of the explanandum. The structure of the explanation parallels that of the predictions that Laws of Nature yield: the explanandum is explained by facts which, if known in advance, would have allowed it to be predicted.

But this analysis of explanation is not adequate as it stands. It makes the criterion of a good explanation the deducibility of the explanandum from true premises by an argument having the following form: Whenever A is the case, B is the case; A was the case; hence B was the case. Now, if whenever A is the case B is the case, it follows that whenever A and Z are both the case B is the case. Applying this conclusion to the explanation above, we can infer from its major premise a law such as the following:

Whenever the temperature of snow rises above 0°C and it is daylight, the snow melts.

Now suppose that, in the case in question, it was indeed daylight when the snow melted. We can now say:

The temperature of the snow rose above 0°C and it was then daylight.

These two assertions can, clearly, function as true premises yielding the conclusion that the snow melted. According to the deductive-nomological model of explanation, they constitute together a good explanation of the melting of the snow, just as good as our original explanation. Yet this is surely not so, for the daylight was irrelevant to the melting of the snow – was no part of its cause, was not a *necessary condition* of it. The deductive pattern of explanation ensures that a sufficient condition of the explanandum is mentioned, but it does not ensure the exclusion of non-necessary conditions. Yet if A is the cause of B, it must be both a necessary and a sufficient condition of B; to say that A caused B is therefore to imply, not one Law of Nature, but two:

Whenever A is the case, B is the case (=A is a sufficient condition of B).
Whenever B is the case, A is the case (=A is a necessary condition of B).

In the case of the melting snow, this means that our explanation implied a second law besides the one already mentioned, namely:

Whenever snow melts, its temperature rises above o°C.

But now we have a new problem. If whenever A is the case B is the case, A cannot be the case unless B is the case. That is, if A is a sufficient condition of B, B is a necessary condition of A; and similarly, if A is a necessary condition of B, B is a sufficient condition of A. But a cause, we saw, is a necessary and sufficient condition of its effect; therefore, the effect is also the necessary and sufficient condition of its cause. The relation between cause and effect appears to be completely symmetrical. The problem, then, is how to distinguish them; for clearly it cannot be done by designating as the cause that which is the necessary and sufficient condition of the other. By that criterion alone, we could as well say (in relation to our example) that the melting of the snow was the cause of its rise in temperature, as vice-versa; which would be absurd. To avoid such absurdity we need to add the element of *chronological order*: a cause always precedes its effect. As Hume pointed out in his classic discussion of causation,[11] the relation of cause and effect is a relation of temporal succession. If A caused B, then whenever A occurs B will occur, and whenever B occurs A has occurred.

Our next task is to distinguish between a relation of cause and effect, and that between two effects of the same cause. If A causes both B and C, then whenever B occurs C occurs and vice versa. B and C might occur simultaneously, or one might precede the other. In the latter case there would be a relation of constant succession between them indistinguishable, on the analysis so far, from a causal relation. The point can be illustrated by successive stages of a disease. For example, victims of measles always develop whitish spots in the mouth (called Koplik's spots) early in the disease. Later, they develop the familiar characteristic rash on the body. The two symptoms are in a relation of

[11] *A Treatise of Human Nature*, Book One, Part III. See especially section II.

constant succession, but neither causes the other – both are caused by infection with the measles virus.

How must we amend our analysis of causation as regular succession to take account of this distinction ? Hume, the originator of this analysis, himself added that cause and effect are *contiguous* in space and time.[12] This seems not to be true of many, perhaps most cases of causation (a tidal wave can be caused by an earthquake hundreds of miles away), but it does perhaps point in the right direction. Where we suspect a causal connection between spatially and temporally separated phenomena, we normally suppose there is a mechanism – a series of spatially and temporally contiguous steps – linking cause and effect. Rom Harré has suggested[13] that we can say that the vibrating of a plucked string causes a sensation of sound only because we know the intervening series of events which links the two phenomena – the movement of air molecules and of various parts of the ear, the electro-chemical changes in the nervous system and the brain. Comparable series of events connect infection with the measles virus to Koplik's spots and to the measles body rash, but not the spots to the rash. We can speak of a relation of cause and effect *either* where cause and effect are spatio-temporally contiguous (as when we say the vibrating of a string causes movement of air molecules, that this in turn makes parts of the ear move, and so on), *or* where they are linked by a continuous series of spatio-temporally contiguous causes and effects (as when we say the vibrating of a string causes sound).

As it stands, this analysis is open to the objection that, in ruling out causal interaction 'at a distance', it would prevent our using causal language in important cases where we normally do so, notably in the case of gravitational attraction. We unhesitatingly believe that distant bodies attract each other despite the absence of any intervening continuous series of causal links. For example, the changing positions of the sun and moon relative to the earth make the earth's oceans move (hence the tides). Admittedly, gravitation is for just this reason a deeply mysterious force; and it is possible that it is mediated by waves travelling through space. But regardless of this there is, we firmly believe, a causal relation between these widely separated movements. We do so, I think, because the motions of bodies (for example the earth's tides) correspond very accurately to predictions based on the Law of Gravitation; and no other way is known of explaining them. We attribute the tides to movements of the sun and moon relative to the earth, because the tides follow these movements with great regularity, and have no known relations of such constant succession with anything else. Here then is a third case in which we can talk of cause and effect, to be added

---

[12] *Ibid.*

[13] In his *Principles of Scientific Thinking* (London, Macmillan, 1970), p. 105.

to the two above: B is caused by A, despite their being at a distance, if A and B stand in a relation of constant succession, and B has no relation of constant succession with any spatio-temporally contiguous phenomenon.

Commonsense and scientific explanation

It follows from our analysis so far that explanation must always be tentative, for it depends on universal laws of succession which cannot be known to be true. If such a law were found to be false, it would seem, any explanation based on it would have to be modified. This gives rise to a problem. Consider once again the example of the melting snow. As a matter of fact, both the laws earlier said to be required for the explanation are false. Under certain circumstances snow will melt at a temperature lower than 0°C, under other circumstances it will not melt till it reaches a temperature higher than 0°C. In other words, it is only under a limited range of conditions that the two laws both hold – that snow melts if and only if its temperature rises above 0°C. In the light of this, can we continue to say that, in our imaginary example, the *cause* of the snow's melting was that its temperature rose above 0°C?

On our analysis of explanation and causation, it would appear not. But common usage suggests otherwise. It admits the idea that a particular sort of event may sometimes cause a given effect and sometimes not. Thus, contact with a 'flu victim can cause 'flu, though it doesn't always do so; similarly, a rise in temperature above a particular level can cause snow to melt, even if it doesn't always do so. But in that case the 'cause' is no longer a sufficient condition of the explanandum: there is no law that enables us to show that, given the 'cause' and only the 'cause' the explanandum could not have been other than it was. In this usage, too, the 'cause' need not be a necessary condition of its effect, since the possibility of different causes of the same effect (such as the melting of snow) is admitted. How, then, if at all, can we justify the common-sense usage as genuinely explanatory?

One possible answer involves so-called probabilistic explanation, relying on a probabilistic (instead of universal) law.[14] This has the form, '*Most* As are B' or 'When A is the case, B is *usually* the case'. On the relative frequency interpretation of probability, it follows from the latter that, if A is the case, B is *probably* the case. Applying this to our original example, we get this deduction:

Major premise: When the temperature of snow rises above 0°C, it usually melts.

[14] Cf. Hempel's (somewhat different) account in *Philosophy of Natural Science*, pp. 58–63.

Minor premise: The temperature of the snow rose above 0°C.

Conclusion: The snow *probably* melted.

Admittedly, the premises of this syllogism do not show that the explanandum could not have been other than it was, but merely that (given only the fact stated in the minor premise) it was more likely than not to have been as it was. It is an attenuated version of Hempel's deductive-nomological explanation, though it approximates more nearly to it the greater the probability of the conclusion. And sometimes, it might be argued, it is the best that can be done.

As a solution to our problem, however, probabilistic explanation will not do, for probabilistic laws are not necessarily involved in common-sense explanations. The cause of a person's getting lung cancer may be that he smoked cigarettes, even though most smokers don't contract the disease. What lies behind the attribution of causation in such a case is, surely, the belief that had the situation been exactly as it was, except that the person did not smoke, he would not have contracted lung cancer, because in such a situation people do not get lung cancer unless they smoke; and that, the situation being as it was, his contracting lung cancer was inevitable, because people in such a situation who smoke always get lung cancer. The 'cause', in other words, is after all in a sense the necessary and sufficient condition of the effect: it is so, in the sort of situation in which it produces the effect. Sometimes, the sort of circumstances in which the 'cause' is a necessary and sufficient condition of the effect can be specified (for example, the melting-point of snow is 0°C if it is pure, at a certain pressure, etc.), but frequently little or nothing is known about them (as in the case of smoking and cancer). What is implied, in a common-sense attribution of causation, is only that there is *some* set of circumstances in which the cause is a necessary and sufficient condition of the effect. Thus, to say that A was the cause of B, is to imply these 'laws':

'Whenever A occurs in some circumstances C, B will occur.'
'Whenever B occurs in some circumstances C, A has occurred.'

From the former of these 'laws', together with the fact that A occurred and the *presumption* that it did so in the appropriate circumstances C (whatever these are), the occurrence of B can be deduced.

Such explanations are perhaps satisfactory at a common-sense level, but from a scientific point of view they are seriously inadequate. In the first place, the laws that they imply are so vague as to be untestable. The first requirement, obviously, is to specify the circumstances in which, allegedly, A and B stand in a relation of constant succession.

The laws can then be tested and, if falsified, altered. But this is not enough. Even if the vague laws are made specific it is possible that a single sort of phenomenon may turn out to have different explanations on different occasions. Thus snow melts at o°C if it is pure and at a certain pressure, but it also melts below o°C if it is at a higher pressure, and so on. There are, in other words, various sets of conditions such that each set is jointly sufficient to make snow melt, but none of which is necessary for it to do so. For science, in contrast to common sense, this is unsatisfactory. Scientific understanding requires that the various explanations be reduced to one, by finding the absolutely necessary and sufficient condition of the explanandum, and relating the various sets of jointly sufficient conditions to it. Thus, the various sets of jointly sufficient conditions for the melting of snow all have in common that where they exist, the snow molecules have sufficient energy to loosen the inter-molecular bonds that hold them together in a regular array when the snow is solid. The cause of snow melting is *always* that its molecules come to have sufficient energy for the bonds between them to be loosened. And if this is so, there are two universal laws that state a relation of constant succession between the advent of this molecular situation and the melting of snow, in terms of which particular meltings can be explained.

Not only particular cases of melting snow can be scientifically explained in this way. So too can other *laws* relating to the melting of snow. Again, the explanations can be put in the form of a deduction, for example:

Major premise: Snow always melts when the energy of its molecules becomes great enough to loosen the inter-molecular bonds that hold them together.

Minor premise: When the temperature of pure snow at atmospheric pressure rises above o°C, its molecules acquire energy great enough to loosen the inter-molecular bonds that hold them together.

Conclusion: When the temperature of pure snow at atmospheric pressure rises above o°C, it melts.

Using the same major premise, laws stating the other conditions under which snow melts can also be deduced. These laws, then, are explained by subsuming them under a *more general* law, of which the explained laws apply to a sub-class of instances. The more general law can in its turn be subsumed under a still more general law, which states the conditions under which solids in general melt, and so on. We saw earlier that the more general a scientific law, the more valued it is. This is because the more general it is, the more phenomena it can explain.

Theoretical terms

We have noted some of the differences between common-sense and scientific explanation, but there is a further difference that calls for comment. The highly general laws involved in scientific explanation make use of specialized terms unknown to common sense – such as 'molecules', in the example above. This gives rise to a problem, which is part of the problem of theoretical terms.[15]

The problem has to do with the requirement that scientific laws must have empirical justification, which in turn requires, we saw, that they be empirically testable. But they frequently employ terms which refer, apparently, to entities – molecules, atoms, electrons, magnetic fields – which are *unobservable*. Another group of theoretical terms refer to so-called *ideal models*, that is, situations or objects that are actually non-existent, such as a perfect vacuum, a frictionless surface, or the point-masses of Newtonian mechanics. Such idealizations are used as simplifying assumptions in working out many basic scientific laws: it is easier to work out the laws of falling bodies on the assumption of a perfect vacuum, for example. But then, laws so derived will hold only in the simplified conditions assumed, which are non-existent, and not in any real situation. How, then, can they be empirically tested? And how, also, can one test empirically laws which purport to describe the behaviour of unobservable entities such as atoms?

The solution to these problems is in principle simple enough. Laws derived from ideal models can be modified to yield laws that apply to real situations – the point of starting from the ideal ones is that it simplifies the task of working out the 'real' laws. Since the 'real' laws are derived from the 'ideal' ones, empirical tests of the former are also tests of the latter. A rather similar solution applies to the unobservable entities: these are scientifically admissible only if they can be systematically related to observation in some way. For example, the laws governing combination of atoms of different elements imply that chemical compounds will yield their component elements in predictable proportions by weight; and this can be empirically tested. Sometimes, the laws relating to unobservable entities may specify that, in certain circumstances, they will betray their existence by interacting with other matter so as to produce observable effects – such as the characteristic tracks left by fundamental particles in cloud chambers and photographic emulsions. Some philosophers, indeed, deny that there is a real distinction between observable and unobservable entities

---

[15] The present discussion owes much to E. Nagel, *op. cit.*, pp. 117–52.

in science – all are observable, though some in less direct ways than others.

Be that as it may, it must be possible, by *combining* laws about so-called unobservables, to deduce observable consequences. Often, in fact, the term 'scientific theory' is reserved for such a structure of deductively connected laws, of which the following would be a fragmentary and rather unspecific example:

(1) The isotope carbon-14 spontaneously emits electrons (Whenever A is the case B is the case).

(2) Electrons leave a characteristic visible track in a cloud chamber (Whenever B is the case C is the case).

Hence (3) if some carbon-14 is placed in a cloud chamber, the characteristic track is produced (∴ Whenever A is the case, C is the case).

Of these three laws only the last is directly testable, but tests of it are indirect tests of the others, for if (3) is false so must be (1) or (2); admittedly we cannot by deductive logic tell which, but there is nothing abnormal about that, for, as we have seen, laws can in general be tested only if other laws can be assumed to hold.

Some philosophers, however, reject the idea that anything can be a scientific statement that is in principle not capable of direct empirical test. On this view, only (3) above is truly a Law of Nature, while (1) and (2) are no more than *formulae* for generating (3). Properly speaking, theoretical laws (or rather formulae) cannot be considered true or false, or as referring to entities such as electrons supposed really to exist – they are simply more or less *useful* in generating empirical laws. Alternatively, it may be held that the *meaning* of a theoretical term such as 'electron' is *identical* with the observable phenomena used as criteria of its existence – this would make (1) above mean, in part, precisely what (3) means, and so an empirical test of (3) would be a *direct* test of (1). ((2) would become tautological.) Both these views must be rejected on the grounds (among others) that they would deprive theoretical laws of what we have seen to be their essential function of *explaining* empirical laws – the former cannot explain the latter if both in fact mean the same. Nor can mere formulae for deriving empirical laws explain these laws – facts can be explained only by facts. We are thus forced to conclude that theoretical entities must be supposed really to exist, and to be distinct from their observable effects – nor have we any reason not to do so.

Reduction

We have seen that in science empirical laws are explained by theoretical laws. We have seen, also, that laws are explained by more general laws. Now, some branches of science are inherently less general than others; biology (the science of living things) has a less general application than physics (the science of all nature), and within physics a theory of gases is less general than a theory of the behaviour of all matter. What exactly is the relation between laws or theories at these different levels of generality? Clearly those of the less general science must be *compatible* with those of the more general – otherwise one or other must be false. One might suppose that, besides, the former must be *derivable* from the latter, that is, explicable in terms of the latter; and that ultimately, everything must be explicable by the most general theories of all, those of fundamental physics. To be sure it is not now possible to derive all scientific theories from basic physics, but there seems every reason to pursue that as an ideal.

Such a view, however, is rejected by many, on the grounds that it overlooks the phenomenon of *emergence*: that is, the fact that at increasingly high levels of organization matter manifests properties *not* deducible from those of matter as such. This claim is frequently put forward on behalf of biology (relative to physics and chemistry), the sciences of human behaviour (relative to all other sciences) and (as we shall see)[16] the social sciences (relative to the science of individual human behaviour). Emergentists deny that it is possible to *reduce* the laws or theories of some particular science to those of another. What, then, does such a reduction involve?

Ernest Nagel, whose discussion of scientific reduction is classic,[17] calls the science that is reduced the secondary science, and the science to which the secondary science is reduced, the primary science. By definition the laws of the primary and secondary sciences use different terms, referring to different entities (otherwise they would not be different sciences), hence the laws of the secondary science can never be simply deduced from those of the primary science. How then can they be reduced to them? The answer is, by establishing a *connection* between the terms (and entities) of the two sciences. As Nagel points out, the well-known reduction of thermodynamics to mechanics in the nineteenth century established *inter alia* that the *temperature* of a gas (a thermodynamic concept) is proportional to the mean *kinetic energy* of its molecules (a mechanical one). Such *connecting laws*, belonging to neither science but establishing a connection between them, make it possible to deduce laws governing the temperature of bodies from the laws of mechanics applied to their constituent molecules. A reduction

---

[16] See below, pp. 75–83, 106–8.　　　　[17] *Op. cit.*, ch. 11.

such as this, which proceeds by treating the entities of the secondary science as wholes made up of parts governed by the laws of the primary science, is often called a *micro-reduction*. It is highly characteristic of scientific reduction. In principle, however, it may be possible to derive laws governing parts from laws governing wholes; and it is quite often asserted, for example, that laws governing the behaviour of parts of biological organisms (organs, cells, and even organic molecules) should be derived from theories about the organisms themselves, rather than vice-versa.[18]

Nagel draws this important conclusion from his analysis: whether a given science is reducible to another is not decidable *a priori*. It depends on whether appropriate connecting laws can be found, and that in turn depends on the terms and laws of the two sciences. As he remarks, thermodynamics could not have been reduced to the mechanics of 1700, given the concepts and laws that it employed. Similarly, chemistry now seems largely reducible to quantum mechanics; it certainly was not reducible to classical mechanics. Nor is it necessarily clear in advance which is to be the primary and which the secondary science – it was only the very reduction of thermodynamics to mechanics that showed the latter to be the more general.

It is clear that reduction of one science to another is also explanation of the secondary science. Indeed, reduction was implicit in our earlier discussion of explanation, for the explanation of the melting of snow in terms of its molecules acquiring sufficient kinetic energy to loosen the bonds holding them together makes use of the reducibility of thermo-dynamics to mechanics. Here again, connecting laws are needed, such as: a solid consists of molecules held together in a regular array by inter-molecular bonds; melting of a solid is the break-up of the regular array of its molecules; when a body's temperature increases the energy of its molecules increases; etc.

[18] See, for example, P. A. Weiss, 'The Living System: Determinism Strati-fied', in A. Koestler and J. R. Smythies (eds), *Beyond Reductionism* (London, Hutchinson, 1969), pp. 3–42.

CHAPTER 2

Minds and Social Science

THE success of the physical sciences, especially physics itself, gives rise to dispute over whether they provide a good model for social science to follow. There seem to be reasons to think so. All sciences, it can plausibly be held, have, almost by definition, basically the same task – to describe and explain phenomena as economically as the facts will allow; hence the model of physics is the model for scientific success in general. On the other hand, physics, unlike the social sciences, does not deal with *people* as such. People of course do have a physical aspect, and considered simply as bodies are as subject to physical laws as any other; but people considered as people behave in ways that cannot (at present, anyway) be derived from these laws. And because the behaviour of people (considered as people) provides the subject-matter of the social sciences, the model of physics is, I believe, inappropriate for them, in several (not all) respects. For people have not only physical bodies, but also (at least according to common belief) conscious *minds*. Whether and in what sense this is true, and whether if true it affects the applicability of the model of physics – differences over these issues are at the root of many controversies in the philosophy of social science.

For social science to exist at all, the first prerequisite is to *identify* its subject-matter, the social. Further basic tasks of social science are to *classify* social phenomena into various kinds, and to *explain* why social phenomena are what they are. I shall argue that all three of these tasks require an approach different from that suggested by the model of physics. In this chapter I shall deal with the first two, leaving explanation till later.

The idea of the social has to do with the fact that human beings relate to one another. These relations manifest themselves in the interdependence of their actions; that a social phenomenon exists implies some pattern of interdependent actions. It follows, then, that identification of the social depends on a prior identification of human action. What does this imply?

Sociological empiricism

Many who would accept the above brief characterisation of the social would hold that the identification and classification of social phenomena should proceed by the same methods of empirical observation that are appropriately used in the physical sciences to identify and classify physical things. Physical scientists take note of such observable features of things as shape, size, position, colour, pitch, loudness, etc. – characteristics perceptible to the senses; social scientists, on this view (which we can label 'sociological empiricism'), should do the same. But if social science is concerned with people, the empiricist view must somehow deal with the phenomena of the human mind – that is, with people's beliefs, desires, purposes, intentions, moral principles, values, etc. – for these appear to be closely connected with their actions (and interactions), but to lack the sorts of characteristics that empiricists consider the only ones science can take note of. Broadly there are two positions open to empiricists here (some seem to hold both, though they are incompatible). Either they may accept that mental phenomena are not empirically observable, and draw the conclusion that social science must completely ignore them, building up its own forms of description and classification on a genuinely scientific (i.e. empirical) basis; or else they may hold that an empiricist social science *can* study mental phenomena, because they *correspond* to overt phenomena (of behaviour) which are open to empirical observation. On the latter view, mental phenomena can be observed, to all intents and purposes, by observing the corresponding overt behaviour; but the typically mental terms normally used to describe them are in principle dispensable because replaceable by terms referring to the corresponding behaviour. Many adherents of both empiricist positions put great stress on the observation of overt behaviour, and can appropriately be called 'behaviourists'.

It is not hard to understand the popularity of such views. The notion of a mind which is not available for inspection by the empirical methods of the physical sciences seems to savour of the occult. If it cannot be so inspected, what can one say about it? Or rather, what can one *not* say about it? What objective check can there be on the validity of accounts of such minds? And if there can be none, how can such accounts be called scientific? It may be that valid knowledge of an empirically unobservable mind is in principle always available to one person – the person whose mind it is; that one knows directly what one's own desires, intentions, beliefs and principles are, even if others have no direct access to them. But this, even if true, would not solve the problem. Science deals with 'public knowledge'.[1] In science the authority of a single individual cannot be accepted; any assertion must be open to

---

[1] To quote the title of a well-known book on the nature of science by the physicist John Ziman (published by Cambridge U.P., 1968).

C

checking by all members of the relevant scientific community. In any case, testimony as to the contents of particular minds from the owners of these minds is often unavailable to social scientists.

Such considerations as these, reinforced by an emotional predilection for the unity of scientific method, have led to a strong current of empiricism among social scientists, especially those who have been self-consciously concerned with the scientific status of their discipline. Thus for Auguste Comte, the originator of the idea of a science of sociology, since science is based on observations of the external world, it can treat individual minds only as physiology or as overt behaviour.[2] The celebrated anthropologist Malinowski endorsed the behaviourist position: for him, 'thoughts', 'beliefs', 'ideas', and 'values' can be introduced into social science only if 'fully defined in terms of overt, observable, physically ascertainable behaviour'.[3] A third prominent exponent of sociological empiricism is Emile Durkheim, highly esteemed as a 'founding father' of modern sociology. Since Durkheim is still much studied, it is worth devoting some attention to the views he expressed in his *Rules of Sociological Method*.

Durkheim insisted on a radical dichotomy between collective 'ways of thinking', and ideas in individual minds; the former are data for the social scientist, the latter are not. His reason for this distinction is partly an empiricist one: collective ways of thinking, unlike the ideas of individuals, can manifest themselves to sensory observation by assuming stable, standardized forms such as written law codes, written creeds, etc. They thereby achieve the status of 'things', as distinct from mere ideas.[4] All 'social facts' are things in this sense. Durkheim writes:

'Social phenomena are things and ought to be treated as things ... All that is subject to observation has thereby the character of a thing ... [Ideas] cannot be perceived or known directly, but only through the phenomenal reality expressing them. We do not know a priori whether ideas form the basis of the diverse currents of social life ... We must therefore consider social phenomena in themselves as distinct from the consciously formed representations of them in the mind; we must study them objectively as external things.'[5]

Hence social facts must be defined and classified in terms of the characteristics that they present to the senses:

[2] Comte's views are quoted and discussed in F. A. Hayek, *The Counter-Revolution of Science* (Glencoe, Free Press Paperback, 1964), p. 172.

[3] B. Malinowski, *A Scientific Theory of Culture* (New York, Oxford U.P., 1960), p. 23.

[4] E. Durkheim, *The Rules of Sociological Method* (Glencoe, Free Press Paperback, 1964), pp. 2–4, 7, 29–30.

[5] *Ibid.*, pp. 27–8.

'Since objects are perceived only through sense perception . . . Science, to be objective, ought to borrow the material for its initial definitions directly from perceptual data.'[6] Thus: 'In order to be objective, the definition [of social facts] must [at first] characterize them by elements external enough to be immediately perceived.'[7]

Although Durkheim does suggest that an empiricist sociology might somehow eventually reveal the importance of ideas in social life, there can be no doubting his negative attitude to ideas, nor that it stems from fear that their unobservability would make a sociology which studied them unreliable – a collection of untestable guesses and prejudices of individual investigators. Often, indeed, it is not clear whether the ideas to which Durkheim takes exception are in the minds of individuals in societies described by sociologists, or in those of the sociologists themselves. Most probably he thinks that sociologists' accounts of ideas in other people's minds will only be ideas about those ideas, rather than statements of fact.

More recently, the empiricist standpoint has been defended with some vigour by the American sociologist, George Lundberg. Lundberg's polemic on the subject is perhaps more impressive as an extreme example of a particular frame of mind than as an argument, but he does raise some important issues, and expresses some representative opinions. Lundberg adheres to both of the incompatible empiricist positions mentioned above. Science, he points out, describes and classifies phenomena in ways which are inevitably different from those of common-sense and pre-scientific ways of thinking, and as it develops continually substitutes new descriptions for old. In this process, says Lundberg, there has been a constant expansion of the 'physical' at the expense of the 'mental'.[8] We could if we wished impute such mental attributes as will and motive to stones or the wind (indeed, it was once common), but it is simply unscientific to do so; similarly with human behaviour. Scientific descriptions must be 'objective', that is, such that different observers agree on the description of a given phenomenon; and mental descriptions are not objective. But in the social sciences the evolution of mental concepts into physical concepts is still incomplete. ' "Will", "feeling", "ends", "motives", "values" etc. . . . are the phlogiston of the social sciences.'[9] In other words, mental concepts belong to an immature stage of social science (as the concept 'phlogiston'

[6] E. Durkheim, *The Rules of Sociological Method*, p. 43.

[7] *Ibid.*, p. 35.

[8] G. A. Lundberg, 'The Postulates of Science and Their Implications for Sociology' in M. Natanson (ed.), *Philosophy of the Social Sciences* (New York, Random House, 1963), pp. 34n., 39–40, 43, 53–4.

[9] *Ibid.*, p. 44.

belonged to an immature stage of chemistry), they are in no sense inherent in social data, and should be replaced by purely physical concepts as quickly as possible.

On the other hand, Lundberg elsewhere disclaims any wish to ignore 'the phenomena of "thought" or "consciousness" '.[10] He admits that 'organisms behave with reference to the anticipated results of behaviour'. However:

> 'Such "ends" whenever they figure in a behaviour situation, exist in the form of symbols of some kind, and organisms respond to these symbols just as they respond to other stimuli. These symbols and whatever they stand for are from our point of view merely part of the data of the situation and have the same power of influencing conduct as any other phenomena that precipitate responses.'[11]

In other words, people's intentions are expressed in *language* (symbols), which is to be studied by the methods of empirical science; for symbolic expressions of ideas and beliefs 'are as observable and objective data as . . . the seasonal flight of birds, or the jump of an electric spark'.[12] Here it is not a question of ridding ourselves of mental concepts, but of finding objective physical expressions of them in observable behaviour, often 'symbolic behaviour' (i.e. speech and writing).[13] Like Durkheim, Lundberg seems to think that an empiricist description of the phenomena will reveal which of them are expressions of ideas.

For more rigorous argument in support of such views, we must turn to philosophers of empiricist leanings. According to one of the most distinguished of the latter, Rudolph Carnap, every term used to describe a mental state is reducible to terms that refer to observable physical things.[14] To ascribe a mental state (such as anger) to a person is equivalent to saying that in given circumstances he will behave in a particular way, and this behaviour, which can be described in *observable thing-terms* (as Carnap calls them), is thus a symptom of the mental state. Like Lundberg, Carnap attaches particular importance to linguistic behaviour, for every mental state has an observable linguistic symptom that can be elicited in appropriate circumstances, namely an utterance of the form 'I am (or was) in mental state Q' (for example 'I am angry') which is describable in physical thing-terms. If a person's being in a particular mental state were not equivalent to his

---

[10] G. A. Lundberg, 'The Postulates of Science and Their Implications for Sociology' in M. Natanson (ed.), *Philosophy of the Social Sciences*, p. 55.
[11] *Ibid.*, p. 34n.   [12] *Ibid.*, p. 53.   [13] *Ibid.*, p. 55.
[14] See his 'Logical Foundations of the Unity of Science' reprinted in L. I. Krimerman (ed.), *The Nature and Scope of Social Science* (New York, Appleton-Century-Crofts, 1969), pp. 362–73, esp. pp. 369–71.

behaving in a certain way in certain circumstances, Carnap holds, it would be impossible to ascribe mental states to other people.

Human action

The tendency of Durkheim, Lundberg and Carnap is to dispense with the mental in favour of the physical. Undoubtedly human beings could be scientifically studied on this basis – but not, I believe, *as* human beings, and certainly not as social beings. This follows from the fact, previously pointed out, that a study of the social relations of men depends on the ability to recognize human action.

How do we find out what people are doing or have done, and how do we describe and classify their actions ? No one would deny that, in an obvious sense, actions can be observed, nor that they present empirically describable characteristics to the observer. When people perform actions their bodies can be seen to move relative to other objects, parts of the body change their spatial orientation and relations, sounds can be heard coming from them, and so on. But this description of the physical aspect of behaviour is clearly not a description of *actions*, of people doing things. Nor could it become one simply by increasing the detail of the physical descriptions – by, for example, giving a phonetic description of the sounds, or a description of the movements in terms of precise measurements. As A. I. Melden has pointed out in a well-known book,[15] an arm rising relative to a body is not the same thing as a man raising his arm, although the former always happens when the latter does. The difference is precisely that between the movement of an object and a human action. Yet, in a sense, both are the very same event – or rather, alternative descriptions of the same event. This is the crux of the matter. In order to see an event as a human action, it is necessary to interpret its empirically observable features in terms of mental categories, to assume the applicability of these categories to what is observed. Only if one assumes that the body whose arm rises is a *man* with intentions, purposes, and desires, and that the rising of his arm is in fact an intentional act of his – only then does one see a man raising his arm.

As several writers have pointed out, it is the purposive aspect of behaviour, not its physical aspects, that constitutes the unity of an action. Consider a rather complex action, such as building a house. This is made up of a number of simpler actions, physically quite disparate (perhaps clearing ground, shaping stones, sawing wood, mixing cement, etc.) and possibly performed discontinuously and even in different places. All of these can be understood as parts of a complex action of house-building only in terms of the agent's purpose in

[15] A. I. Melden, *Free Action* (London, Routledge and Kegan Paul, 1961), esp. chs. VI and XIII.

performing them. Equally, similar simple actions can belong to quite different complex actions: in sawing wood one may be building a house or preparing a fire, and it is the sawer's purpose, not his overt movements, that distinguishes the one from the other.

Against this analysis, it might be argued that the so-called purposive aspect of behaviour is, after all, discoverable by empirical observation, without any need to postulate a conscious mind 'behind' the behaviour. The idea, in brief, is that the purpose of behaviour is the end result that it tends to bring about. Thus, we could recognize the various movements involved in building a house as parts of that complex action by their tendency to bring the house into existence; we could recognize wood-sawing movements as part of preparing a fire, again, by observing the fire resulting from them. This approach tends to deny any major discontinuity between human behaviour and that of non-human entities such as animals and even machines. Certainly it seems natural to attribute actions to animals even though we cannot be sure they have conscious intentions; and it seems, too, that we do so in terms of the results their behaviour tends to bring about. Thus, Charles Taylor has argued[16] that even the responses taught to animals by behaviourist psychologists must be considered to be actions, not mere movements – rats, for example, learn to lower a lever, an *action* corresponding to *different* movements in different circumstances (the rat may use its paws or its teeth, etc.), the constant factor in what is learnt being precisely the end result that these movements tend to bring about. Even instinctive behaviour of lowly animals, such as the nest-building behaviour of wasps, manifests this characteristic. And so can that of machines, which may be so constructed as to tend to bring about a certain state of affairs, and in so doing to adjust their behaviour to circumstances. Communication theorists such as Wiener and Rosenblueth have suggested that this is precisely the nature of purposive behaviour;[17] just as a guided missile seeks out a target by continually adjusting its flight in the light of information about its position relative to the target, so a person who picks up a cup adjusts the position and orientation of his hand in the light of information about its position relative to the cup, in such a way that the cup is picked up. This goal-directedness of behaviour constitutes its purposiveness and, so to speak, its 'action-ness', and purposive human action is thus assimilated to the behaviour of animals and machines.

[16] C. Taylor, *The Explanation of Behaviour* (London, Routledge and Kegan Paul, 1964), pp. 204–6, 211–12.

[17] See A. Rosenblueth, N. Wiener, and J. Bigelow, 'Behaviour, Purpose, and Teleology', *Philosophy of Science*, vol. X (1943) pp. 18–24; N. Wiener, *The Human Use of Human Beings* (London, Sphere Books, 1968), pp. 23–7. See also Rosenblueth and Wiener, 'Purposeful and Non-Purposeful Behaviour', *Philosophy of Science*, vol. 17 (1950), pp. 318 ff., and the 'Rejoinder' by R. Taylor.

This argument is not really convincing. The purpose of an action is indeed the goal to which it is directed, but this cannot be identified with the result it brings about. The two coincide only if the agent, first, *believed* (correctly) that his movements would have that result, and, second, *desired* that that result should come about. Neither of these conditions necessarily holds – people make mistakes, fail to achieve the results they expect, and bring about results quite unforeseen; and even correctly foreseen results of their actions may not be desired results, but rather costs they are willing to incur for the sake of some other goal. That people's behaviour is goal-directed implies that they have certain desires and beliefs in mind. The mere tendency of a process to produce a specifiable result is not sufficient ground to invoke the concept of action (or purpose). As is well known, biological organisms tend to maintain themselves in particular states through homeostatic processes – but it would be absurd to call these automatic processes actions, or to suppose that they revealed purposes. The purpose or intention that guides an action is something that characterizes the agent before and while he acts, not the result he brings about. If we attribute actions to animals we must either suppose they have intentions in something like the human sense (as might perhaps be true of rats) or else we use the term in a sense different from that which is relevant to human agency.

Even if the result of an action always conformed to its purpose, the empiricist case would not be much helped, because an intended result is not necessarily characterizable in purely empirical terms. Suppose a man (intentionally) casts a vote by marking a cross on a ballot paper. The empirical consequence of his action is that there is a cross on a bit of paper, but the intended result, in terms of which his action is to be characterized, is that he has cast a vote. An empirically identical action and result would not constitute casting a vote without the necessary background of functioning rules that constitute the institution of voting.[18] This example is in fact a specifically social sort of action, and thus introduces a topic that requires fuller consideration.

Social action

Not all human actions fall within the purview of the social sciences. According to Max Weber, another of the 'founding fathers', these sciences attempt to understand and explain 'social action', which he defines as follows:

'In "action" is included all human behaviour when and insofar as the acting individual attaches a subjective meaning to it. . . . Action is social insofar as, by virtue of the subjective meaning attached to it

[18] Cf. P. Winch, *The Idea of a Social Science* (London, Routledge and Kegan Paul, 1958), pp. 45–51.

by the acting individual (or individuals), it takes account of the behaviour of others.'[19]

He goes on:

'The term "social relationship" [denotes] the behaviour of a plurality of actors insofar as, in its meaningful content, the action of each takes account of that of others and is oriented in these terms.'[20]

Weber's definition of action is very much in accord with the notion of action developed above, for his concept of behaviour to which the agent attaches a 'subjective meaning' is pretty much the same as that of purposive behaviour. Social action, then, is, on Weber's definition, action conditioned by the agent's *subjective awareness* of other people's behaviour, and a social *relationship*, in turn, involves a reciprocal social awareness on the part of several people. It follows that, in order to identify social actions and social relationships, the observer must not only interpret the empirically describable features of behaviour in terms of a set of mental categories, he must attribute to the people involved a specific sort of mental orientation, namely an awareness of *others* as *people* having intentions, purposes, desires, etc. Not only must the social scientist be able to recognize human actions, he must suppose that those whose actions he studies can do so too.

Although on Weber's account the social sciences are concerned with only a particular category of actions, all human actions are to some extent a social product. Man is a social animal. A person's intentions and purposes, his very capacity to have intentions and purposes, depend on his experience of social relationships, especially those of early childhood. Peter Winch has drawn attention to a particular sense in which all human actions depend on the social, a sense which is highly relevant to the present context.[21] It has to do with the way in which a person is able to attach what Weber calls a 'subjective meaning' to his behaviour. That behaviour is subjectively meaningful implies that the agent has a conception, under some particular description, of what the purpose or point of the behaviour is – he could (assuming he possesses the normal means of expression) describe its point, and thus the nature of the action as he conceives it. 'Building a house' would be one such description of the nature of an action, corresponding to the agent's conception of the point of the behaviour involved. That the agent has such a conception implies that he understands a *language* which includes some expression equivalent in meaning to 'building a house'. But language is, of course,

[19] M. Weber, *The Theory of Social and Economic Organization* (Glencoe, Free Press Paperback, 1964), p. 88.
[20] *Ibid.*, p. 118.   [21] See footnote 18 above.

a *social* institution: it is a set of conventions shared by a social group, by virtue of which meanings are attached to sounds and marks (words). Thus, a person's attaching a particular subjective meaning to his action depends on his belonging to a community whose language includes appropriate concepts.

Whether the social scientist, in classifying actions in which he is interested, must use the same description as the agent would use, is a vexed question consideration of which can be postponed. But it seems clear that a grasp of the agent's own understanding of his action is essential to a scientific understanding of it.

Language

It is by now evident (and is not in any case very controversial) that a social scientist's knowledge of what goes on in a community depends on an understanding of its language. Indeed, the amount of actual observation of action that social scientists perform is relatively small – they are to a large extent dependent on linguistic *accounts* of action, both written and oral. Political scientists, for example, do not observe Cabinet meetings – their knowledge of them is derived from linguistic descriptions by participants of what (purportedly) happened in them; nor do they observe how electors vote – they depend on linguistic information supplied by the electors. Again, criminologists rarely observe crimes being committed – what they know about the numbers and types of crimes rests largely on official enumerations, which in turn are based on linguistic reports. All sorts of social scientists depend on linguistic information given in reply to questionnaires. Perhaps the only social scientists who habitually *observe* their subject matter are social anthropologists, and those who study small groups; and even they, obviously, must take account of their subjects' use of language. This means that they must either themselves understand their subjects' language, or rely on the translations of those who do. As has often been pointed out, the experience of anthropologists in unfamiliar communities gives the lie to any idea that the identification of actions is in principle a straightforward matter, simply requiring careful observation of the physical characteristics that social life presents to the observer. On the contrary, it takes a considerable time before these manifestations become comprehensible as particular sorts of actions; and they do so as the anthropologist acquires knowledge of the group's language, which is both an essential part of their social life and a means of questioning participants about that life.

Language is in many ways the quintessential social phenomenon. Human social life is inconceivable without it, and it is itself a social institution. It is therefore very pertinent to assess the empiricist programme for social science in the light of the social scientist's inescapable need to understand language. We have seen that empiricists such as Lundberg and Carnap themselves stress the importance of language; they maintain, however, that it is an empirical datum to be studied like any other. Language does of course present certain empirical characteristics to the observer – certain sounds, marks on paper or other surfaces, puffs of smoke rising from a fire, etc. But to recognize these phenomena *as* language is already to have gone beyond empirical description. Sounds, marks, and smoke as such are not linguistic phenomena: they become so through the *conventions* of particular social groups. Here the ancient distinction between nature and convention is very much to the point. To describe people as using language (speaking, writing, etc.) is not simply to describe them as making sounds or marks: it is, in addition, to attribute certain mental characteristics both to the speaker or writer, and to the members of his linguistic community in general.[22] A man is not speaking unless he *intends*, by making certain sounds, to convey a certain meaning to others; and if he is to succeed in this, the latter must share with him an *awareness* of a certain conventional meaning attributed to those sounds by a linguistic community to which both speaker and hearers belong.

The inadequacy of an empiricist treatment of language becomes even clearer, perhaps, if we consider how a social scientist can know, not just that people are using language, but what exactly they are saying, that is, what their words mean. Clearly, there need be no empirical resemblance between words and what they mean – compare a cat with the word 'cat', for example. The word, indeed, has both a spoken and a written form, which empirically have no resemblance to one another. Consider, too, the cat's zoological name '*felis domesticus*', which again has no physical resemblance, in either its spoken or written form, to either form of the word 'cat'. All these linguistic units are equivalent; but they can be classified as similar only on the basis of their similar *meaning*, not of any empirical similarity. Any attempt to understand language on the basis of the physical characteristics of the words used is absurd.

How, then, does the social scientist or anyone else learn a language if he doesn't already know it? A rather desperate empiricist argument asserts that the meaning of the words is (or could be) learnt by observing correlations between the utterance of particular sounds and the presence of particular things. Thus, one might learn what the sound 'cat' means by hearing it repeatedly spoken when a cat is present. Babies, and those who must learn an unknown language without a teacher, doubtless do learn at least partly in this way. However, anyone who got no further than noticing a correlation of sound and object would not have under-

---

[22] The account of language given here owes much to R. M. Chisolm, 'Sentences about Believing', reprinted in L. I. Krimerman (ed.), *op. cit.*, pp. 398–408.

stood that 'cat' is a word as distinct from a response to a stimulus. To grasp this fact it is necessary to realize that it is a sound people make when they *intend* to convey something about a certain sort of object (a cat), which in fact need not be present. It is impossible to learn a language without interpreting what is observed in terms of mental categories.

The significance of language specifically for the social scientist should not be misunderstood. The physical scientist, too, obviously needs to understand language in order to do his job. He belongs to a scientific community which uses its own specialized language to convey information about experiments, propose theories, etc. If he is interested in particular past events, such as earthquakes, eclipses, etc., that may have occurred centuries ago, he will have to depend on accounts by earlier, possibly non-specialist observers. Should these accounts pose problems of interpretation, he will have to call on experts who are specialists in meaning – historians, linguists, etc. (or else become one himself). As for the linguistic intercourse within his own profession, the physical scientist's unproblematical understanding of this illustrates the fact that everyone is to some extent a social scientist *sans le savoir*. Everyone who participates in social life necessarily knows a good deal about the institutions of his society, in particular its language – things which an alien social scientist would have to learn. Thus the physical scientist knows a lot about the institutions of his professional community that might have to be learned by a sociologist or anthropologist of science. But the crucial difference between the physical and the social scientist is that only the latter studies a subject-matter of which a language is an essential element, and which cannot be understood unless that language is understood.

Knowledge of a community's language enables a social scientist to *question* its members. This is a privilege denied to physical scientists, but one which must, as is well known, be used with care, for it gives rise to the possibility of *misunderstanding*, perhaps especially where the investigator might be tempted to suppose that he and his subject-matter share exactly the same language. Social scientists who use questionnaires have frequently got into trouble through mistakenly supposing that, for example, manual workers understand relatively abstract terms like 'class' in the same way as they themselves do.[23] This of course reinforces the general lesson that the social scientist has to understand the subjective meaning of language to its user – not just observe its empirical characteristics. But usually it will not be enough for the social scientist just to understand his respondent's meaning:

[23] Another example is given in H. P. Rickman, *Understanding and the Human Studies* (London, Heinemann, 1967), p. 68.

social scientists normally wish to use respondents' assertions that something is the case as *evidence* that it in fact is. Assuming that a respondent has the necessary knowledge to give correct information, this involves also a judgement about his state of *mind* – i.e. that he wishes to convey that information in his response. This, of course, need not be so – many respondents may have motives for misleading the questioner. The physical scientist, though he too may have difficulties in interpreting his observations, need not worry that his subject-matter may by trying to deceive him.

The meaning of language is not only an essential clue to what people are doing and the vehicle of reports about what they have done, it is also often itself the direct object of sociological interest. Language can, for example, express *beliefs* which are widespread in particular social groups; and the concern of the so-called sociology of knowledge is, precisely, to relate systems of beliefs to their social context. Just how to characterize a particular belief can, however, be a considerable problem. A famous case in point is the puzzling saying current among the Nuer (studied by Evans-Pritchard) apparently to the effect that human twins are birds.[24] There has been much controversy as to just what this statement actually *means* (in other words, what the Nuer really believe). Should its English translation be taken literally, or metaphorically or 'symbolically'? Is English perhaps simply unable to render the sense it has in the indigenous language? Be that as it may, the social phenomenon that the controversy is about is a phenomenon of meaning and nothing else. So too are those social phenomena constituted by abstract belief-systems – scientific theories, religious creeds, moral codes, systems of philosophy, etc. In so far as the social scientist is interested in these as theories rather than for any practical application they may have, they are accessible to him only through the language (usually writing) in which they are expressed. Despite Durkheim, it is of course not possible to understand them by subjecting the writing to empirical study.

Social institutions
Prominent among the phenomena studied by social scientists are *social institutions*. A social institution is a complex of rules relating to an area of social relations. Broadly, the rules may be *enabling* or *obliging* or both; that is, they may provide ways in which people can co-operate so as to achieve some result, and they may also oblige them to do (or not do) certain things. It scarcely needs to be said that, for an institution

[24] For discussions of Evans-Pritchard's *Nuer Religion*, see Ernest Gellner, 'Concepts and Society' in B. R. Wilson (ed.), *Rationality* (Oxford, Blackwell, 1970), pp. 34–9, and J. Littlejohn, 'Twins, Birds, etc.', *Bijdragen tot de Taal-, Land-en Volkenkunde*, Deel 126 (1970), pp. 92–114.

to function, those involved must *know* what the rules are, and must *expect* one another to keep more or less to the rules. Language is not only involved in all social institutions, it is itself a social institution, a complex of rules of meaning and grammar (as such it is the province of a certain sort of social scientist – the linguist). Some other institutions involve language in a special way, such that the use of language has by convention a specific social significance.[25] For example, the social institutions of promising and of contract are essentially linguistic, in the sense that by the rules of these institutions the uttering of words according to certain forms gives rise to specific rights and obligations. To describe such phenomena a social scientist must understand what these utterances mean to the social group, both in the semantic sense, and in the sense of the social expectations conventionally founded on them.

Not only the uttering of words, but any action whatever can acquire a particular social significance through institutional conventions. This is a further reason why an empiricist account of social phenomena would miss the point. Even if actions as such could be correctly identified in a purely empiricist way (which anyway is not the case, as we have seen), they could not in that way be identified as belonging to social institutions. To revert to Melden's famous example,[26] someone raising his arm may or may not be *giving a signal*, depending, not only on his own intentions, but on the conventions of the relevant community as to what constitutes a signal. Empirically similar actions may constitute quite different *social* actions in consequence of the relevant institutional rules – raising one's arm may be not only signalling, but also saluting, casting a vote, etc. Conversely, empirically quite different actions may be socially equivalent – one casts a vote sometimes by raising one's arm, sometimes by marking a cross on paper. An empiricist, even supposing he could identify these phenomena as actions, would be more likely to classify raising the arm in salute and in voting as the same sort of action, than to classify voting by arm-raising and by cross-marking as the same. Needless to say, that would be absurd.

Social institutions are extremely important to the sociologist. The description of any society must include description of its major institutions – of marriage, property, government, religion, etc. But institutions, it is now clear, are not observable in an empiricist way. The same is true of another important social phenomenon, the *organization*, which exists only through institutions. A group of men talking round a table can constitute (say) a meeting of a company's board of directors only by virtue of a complex of background rules and conventions.

[25] Cf. A. Ryan, *The Philosophy of the Social Sciences* (London, Macmillan, 1970), p. 133, on J. L. Austin's *How to Do Things with Words*.
[26] *Op. cit.*, pp. 18–21, 190–1.

Some consequences of empiricism in social science

Whichever way one turns in the social sciences, one finds that the phenomena with which social scientists typically try to deal are not suited to the empiricist approach, but require the social scientist to assume certain mental operations on the part of the people he studies. Yet social scientists often seem to wish to avoid such assumptions. I want now to illustrate the dangers of so doing by considering two examples from the work of contemporary social scientists.

The first example relates to the phenomenon of *power*, which is of prime concern to political scientists. According to Robert Dahl, writing in the *International Encyclopaedia of the Social Sciences*,[27] 'C has power over R' means 'C's behaviour causes R's behaviour'. This definition shows the influence of empiricism in that it avoids any overt reference to anyone's mental state. For this very reason it is wrong. If C's behaviour causes R to punch him on the nose, this hardly shows that C has power over R. As Stanley Benn has pointed out,[28] C has power over R only to the extent that R's behaviour approximates to what C *intends* (or *wants*) it to be. And usually, when C exercises power over R, the latter's behaviour is not caused by brute force, but is a deliberate action more or less influenced by circumstances controlled by C (as when one hands over money in response to a gunman's threat). Power relations between people normally operate through the mind, not the body.

My second example is drawn from the avowedly behaviourist (i.e. empiricist) theory of the sociologist George Homans.[29] In this theory the basic terms are 'activities' and 'sentiments'. But 'sentiments' are not what one might think; they are a particular class of 'activities', namely 'activities that the members of a particular verbal or symbolic community say are signs of the attitudes and feelings a man takes towards another man or other men'. They are not the unobservable attitudes and feelings themselves, but 'directly observable' behavioural expressions of them, for example thanking and kissing, which in some societies conventionally express love. To call such behaviour 'sentiments' might seem merely odd, but what is worse, it leads to confusion and self-contradiction. Thus, a 'sentiment' to which Homans attaches particular importance, because of its effects on behaviour, is social approval – which is of course an attitude, not an activity. Perhaps for Homans the term 'social approval' is shorthand for 'conventional behavioural expressions of social approval'? Apparently not: for the

[27] Vol. 12, p. 410 (in article 'Power', pp. 405–15).
[28] In the *Encyclopaedia of Philosophy*, Vol. 6, p. 426 (in article 'Power', pp. 424–7).
[29] See his *Elementary Social Behaviour* (London, Routledge and Kegan Paul, 1961), pp. 33–4.

effect that such expressions have on the behaviour of another person depends, as Homans admits, on whether they are perceived by him as *sincere*. If not, 'the sentiment would be another sentiment'. It seems, then, that two identical pieces of overt behaviour may be (or express) quite different 'sentiments', depending on whether another person *believes* that the 'behaver' does or does not *intend* to deceive him (that is, make him *believe* what is false). The attempt to avoid having to do with unobservable mental states has not only caused terminological confusion, it has completely failed.

Unobservables and explanation

I have argued that the model of physics is inapplicable in the social sciences because the existence of social facts always implies the existence of mental states – intentions, purposes, beliefs, expectations, awareness of rules – which are not observable by empirical methods. It is, however, possible to accept the premise without accepting the conclusion. After all, physics too deals with unobservable phenomena, namely the theoretical entities discussed in the previous chapter, such as electrons, magnetic fields, etc.[30] Do not our mental phenomena, perhaps, have a similar status to these ? The theoretical entities of physics, we concluded, are to be considered as real entities capable of causing empirical phenomena. Thus, an observed phenomenon (such as a track in a cloud chamber) can be explained using a law (or laws) concerning the effects of interaction of unobservable entities of a particular sort (such as electrons) with other sorts of matter. If mental entities such as intentions and purposes were comparable to these theoretical physical entities, they would be capable of causing certain empirically observable phenomena, and would have lawful connections with them similar to those between electrons and tracks in cloud chambers.

But even if this were the case, it would not follow that mental states have a similar status in the social sciences to that of the theoretical entities in physical science. The empirical phenomena caused by mental states would be, presumably, bodily movements. There might, for example, be a causal connection between the intention to raise one's arm, and the rising of one's arm. Social science is not, however, interested in bodily movements like the rising of arms, nor in any possible causal connections between these movements and mental states. It is interested in the description and explanation of (social) *actions*, and these cannot (unlike the observable effects of theoretical entities) be described in purely physical terms. The significance of mental states for the social sciences is, in the first place, not to explain bodily movements, but to constitute a framework of concepts in terms of which these movements can be understood as actions.

[30] See above, pp. 28–9.

This is not to say that mental states are not involved in the explanation of actions and of movements. Indeed, it is obvious that intentions, purposes, etc., *are* involved in the explanation of actions and, since actions involve movements, mental states could be said to be indirectly involved in the explanation of movements through their role in explaining actions. The question then arises whether mental states cause actions in the same sort of way as electrons cause tracks in cloud chambers – whether, that is, their explanatory force in relation to actions derives from causal laws linking particular kinds of mental states with particular kinds of actions. This is a very large question, which will have to be treated at length in a later chapter on explanation in the social sciences.[31]

[31] Below, pp. 83–106.

CHAPTER 3

Regularities in Social Science

WE have seen that physical science aims above all to establish laws, and that its explanations depend on them. Before considering social explanation we will examine the idea of *social laws*; for whether such laws exist, at any rate in a form comparable to physical laws, is a controversial matter. We can then (in chapter 4) discuss a separate controversy: the relation between laws and explanation in social science.

Social laws and laws of historical succession
Let us first clarify the expression 'social laws'. Popper, who believes that the role of laws is essentially the same in physical and social science,[1] stresses a distinction between genuine scientific laws of society and a sort of pseudo-laws, namely historical 'laws' of succession.[2] The latter state allegedly necessary successive stages of development, either of society as a whole or of particular institutions (political, religious, etc.). The stages sometimes constitute a pattern of cyclical recurrence, sometimes a trend in a specified direction – as in the theories of Marx, Comte and Spencer. In physical science, Popper says, there are no laws of succession. To be sure, many predictable standard sequences of events occur in the world: animals are born, mature, age, and die; stars evolve through predictable stages; night and day alternate on earth and other planets. But no one sequence of this kind is the unfolding of a single law; rather it *depends* on (usually) several laws, together with the persistence of appropriate conditions (the alternation of day and night on earth depends on the laws of gravitation and light, and specific facts about the earth and sun). Should these conditions change, as is perfectly possible, the standard sequences will change too (as often happens to animals).

[1] K. R. Popper, *The Poverty of Historicism* (London, Routledge and Kegan Paul paperback, 1961), p. 62 and pp. 97–103.
[2] *Ibid.*, pp. 105–30.

D

What about the theory of biological evolution? Is it not a law of succession? Rather, says Popper, it is a description of a unique sequence, the evolution of life on earth, and is thus a *singular historical statement*, dependent on many laws. It describes the relations of biological forms, much as a human genealogy might describe those of individuals. It is thus not a law about all processes of a particular kind, corroborable by particular instances; and the same is true of social 'laws' of succession, since they too are really descriptions of a unique sequence – namely, the evolution of human society. Despite Popper, the theory of biological evolution *can* be stated as a corroborable law, roughly as follows: 'All earthly organisms are biologically related' (not of course directly). But this is not a law *of succession* – it does not specify the successive phases of evolution.

There is, however, one very important physical law of succession. The second law of thermodynamics states that *entropy* (i.e. randomness) continually increases up to a maximum in all closed systems. Hence, regardless of particular conditions, the total entropy of the universe always increases until the maximum is reached. This is a law describing a unique historical sequence – the history of universal entropy – yet it is in principle corroborable by particular instances. The reason is that it can *also* be expressed as a universal law: 'at any instant universal entropy is as great or greater than at every previous instant'. Any social law of succession which, like the universal entropy law, specified an increasing and irreversible trend, would be similarly corroborable. Other social laws of succession, if they referred to a particular society or 'society' in general, would deserve Popper's strictures; but if they referred to *all* societies, they would be universal in form and in principle corroborable by instances.[3] Whether any such law is actually well corroborated is of course another matter.

Indeed, it is questionable whether social life is at all amenable to description in terms of laws modelled on those of physical science. For both theoretical and practical reasons, the search for social science laws is widely and vigorously prosecuted, yet it seems relatively unsuccessful. Let us now consider whether this reflects some inherent intractability of social life to such an enterprise.

Cross-cultural generalization

The entire physical universe is (physicists believe) everywhere and always essentially the same, in the sense that it is made up of the same (relatively few) fundamental particles governed by the same (few) sorts of force (electromagnetic, gravitational and nuclear forces). Hence

[3] Cf. Q. Gibson, *The Logic of Social Enquiry* (London, Routledge and Kegan Paul, 1960), p. 195n.

physical laws can be very widely applicable in space and time (for example, the Law of Gravitation). But the social universe appears not to be like this. Social forms (like biological forms) are limited to particular times and places. Such institutions as modern-style trade unions and political parties are found only in modern societies, which however lack such institutions as, say, the oracles that flourished in earlier cultures. This does not rule out laws – universal or statistical – relating to trade unions, political parties, or oracles, but such laws would have a relatively limited application.

Social science does not differ from biology or such physical sciences as astronomy and geology in using concepts having only a local relevance. The question is, however, whether social science is *confined* to such concepts, or whether the social universe can legitimately be described by concepts having a *cross-cultural* application. Can localized institutions such as trade unions or political parties be considered as instances of broader phenomena that might be found in any society? Or can they be treated, analogously with physical and biological phenomena, as consisting of relatively few 'elements' recurrent in all sorts of societies? Some writers have objected in principle to any kind of cross-cultural social concepts, and thus to cross-cultural generalizations. Peter Winch, for example, has been widely interpreted in this sense.

There is no doubt that Winch objects to some efforts of social scientists to construct cross-cultural categories.[4] Thus, Pareto (his main target) is taken to task for treating as similar (i.e. putting in the same category) first, the relation between 'an American millionaire and a plain American' and that between high- and low-caste Indians; and second, Christian baptism and pagan rites involving sprinkling of lustral water. Winch's objections appear to rule out *all* cross-cultural social categories. He argues that to treat two things as similar or different depends on adopting criteria of similarity and difference. How are these criteria to be determined? According to Winch, social 'things' depend for their existence on the way of life of a specific community, and on *its criteria* of similarity and difference. Thus, it is Christians who are the qualified experts on what actions count as Christian baptism, and therefore on what actions are 'similar' to baptism. In fact, Winch seems to hold, they cannot count any non-Christian activity as similar to Christian baptism, because no such activity is part of the Christian way of life, and the nature of a social phenomenon derives from its place in a specific way of life.

But this is a confusion. It is true that 'baptism' is a (Christian) religious concept and the question 'is x baptism?' must be answered by

[4] *Op. cit.*, pp. 86–90, 103–8.

(Christian) religious criteria. Pagan lustral rites are *not* baptism. But whether they are the same kind of thing as baptism is another question entirely – one to which no absolute answer can be given. Two things are never, as Winch rightly notes, either similar or different in themselves; rather, they normally have both similarities and differences (a rock and a table are different in obvious ways, but are similar in being both material bodies – so that the Law of Gravitation applies to both). Baptism and lustral rites are obviously similar in that both are religious rites involving the use of water for symbolic purification. Whether this similarity is *significant*, as Pareto thought, is another question, but no reason is apparent why *no* similarity of social phenomena belonging to different cultures could ever be significant. Is it not significant that American and Indian society are both *stratified* (unequal)? Yet if Pareto's comparison of American class differences and Hindu caste differences is *a priori* illegitimate, we could not even say this. Some sociologists believe that *all* societies are stratified (a universal law). Winch's argument has the absurd result that this law is not false (which it may well be), but meaningless. Winch must also deny, it seems, that very different (perhaps all) societies have in common such broadly defined institutions as religion, money, exchange, the family, even language – which would be extremely strange.

We can in fact turn Winch's own argument upside down. Winch emphasizes that the social scientist has to be able to identify behaviour as *social*, that is, as part of the shared way of life of a human group, dependent on the group's shared concepts and meanings. But to say of two items of behaviour occurring in different groups that both are 'social' implies that the groups are similar in that they manifest the characteristics of human social life. The concepts 'social' and 'society', if there is more than one society, are necessarily cross-cultural. In recognizing an alien society, the investigator necessarily recognizes some similarity to his own society and therefore can, in principle, categorize phenomena in the two as similar.[5]

Social generalizations and their shortcomings
If cross-cultural concepts are legitimate, sociological laws applicable to different societies may be possible. But although many social science laws have been formulated, there is considerable dissatisfaction and dubiety about their status. Let us use a few such laws to illustrate this. The largest and most impressive group of such laws are the laws of economics, such as the following:

(1) Under conditions of perfect competition, the price of each com-

[5] Cf. F. A. Hayek, *op. cit.*, pp. 75–7, on the related problem of 'cross-historical' categories.

modity is equal to the marginal cost of production for each firm that produces it.

(2) An increase in government expenditure relative to taxation increases aggregate demand and thereby reduces unemployment or raises prices.

Then there are laws of Marxist provenance; such as:

(3) In all societies in which the means of production are privately owned, the owners of the means of production constitute a ruling class, which eventually loses power in a revolution led by another ('ascendant') class.

(4) In all societies in which the means of production are socially owned class conflict and the state disappear.

Let us add the following laws, of heterogeneous origin:[6]

(5) All societies are ruled by an oligarchy.

(6) All societies are stratified.

(7) All societies have incest taboos.

(8) In industrial societies consumers' pressure-groups are never as effectively organized as some producers' pressure-groups.

(9) Revolution is impossible unless the ruling class is weakened by internal dissension or defeat in war.

We saw in chapter 1 that two virtues of scientific laws are precision and generality of scope. In these respects social science laws compare badly with physics. Two sorts of imprecision afflict social science, a lack respectively of *specificity* and of *clarity*. Thus all the above laws except the first two and the seventh are somewhat unclear in their meaning – one knows only roughly, not precisely, what counts as a 'ruling class', 'class conflict', an 'oligarchy', a 'stratified society', a 'revolution'. Lack of specificity appears in the fact that only the first law is an exact quantitative law comparable (in this respect) to, say, the Law of Gravitation, and indeed outside economics such laws are practically unknown in social science. The second law is only an approximate quantitative law – while clear enough in meaning it fails to specify any exact relation between the quantities involved. Many of the other laws may be called 'vaguely quantitative', and it is this that gives rise to their unclarity. Thus, the eighth law implies quantitative comparison of the effectiveness of pressure-groups, while concepts such as 'ruling class' and 'oligarchy' imply quantitative comparison of the power of various groups; but *how* these phenomena are to be compared

---

[6] Law (5) is associated with 'élite theorists' such as Gaetano Mosca, Vilfredo Pareto, and especially Robert Michels; laws (6) and (7) are cited in G. C. Homans, *The Nature of Social Science* (New York, Harcourt, Brace and World, 1967), pp. 30–1; laws (8) and (9) are asserted by K. R. Popper in *The Poverty of Historicism*, p. 62.

is far from clear. The concepts 'ruling class', 'oligarchy' and 'stratified society' also imply some degree of *difference* in the power or wealth of different groups, but fail to specify how much. Similarly, concepts such as 'revolution' imply, but do not specify, some minimum *magnitude* of social change.

As for generality of scope, while the range of applicability possible for a social science law is obviously much less than in physics, even within the social universe the degree of generality achieved seems on the whole slight. True, laws (5), (6) and (7) above refer to 'all societies'. But laws such as (1), (2) and (8) which apply only in certain sorts of social systems are much more typical of the social sciences (despite the fact that, as we saw, there is no objection in principle to cross-cultural concepts). In social science, precision and generality seem normally to be alternatives[7] – they are rarely combined in any high degree (unlike in physics). Thus, both the genuinely quantitative laws in our list (excluding, that is, the 'vaguely quantitative') are limited in application to a particular sort of social system.

If generality can be bought by sacrificing precision, it can sometimes also be bought by sacrificing *universality* (and vice-versa). Law (5) for example, like the other laws in the list, is stated in universal form, but it may well be doubted whether, in this form, it is true. If not, it may still be true as a *probabilistic* law, that is, a law which applies, not to all cases of a given type, but to the bulk of such cases. A probabilistic law is a particular sort of statistical law. Statistical laws, we saw,[8] have the form 'x% of As are Bs'; in probabilistic laws, x is high, but less than 100. The higher x is, the 'more universal' the law. But in social science, probabilistic laws are usually unspecific – rarely if ever is the numerical value of x specified, in marked contrast with the exact statistical laws of quantum mechanics. Law (5) re-stated probabilistically, would thus assert:

'Most (or perhaps, the great majority of) societies are ruled by an oligarchy.'

Now, it might be possible to predicate a *more universal* law of oligarchic rule about a *less general* subject, i.e. some relatively particular kind of society, instead of societies in general:

'Societies that are predominantly but not wholly illiterate are *almost always* ruled by an oligarchy.'

Truly universal laws, however, which are well corroborated and to

---

[7] Cf. P. S. Cohen, *Modern Social Theory* (London, Heinemann, 1968), p. 8.
[8] Above, p. 19.

which no exceptions are known, and which are of any significant degree of generality, are rare indeed in social science. Many social science laws are both merely probabilistic and of very restricted scope, referring perhaps, in extreme (but not rare) cases, to only one society over a limited span of its history – for example the following:

'In contemporary Britain most trade unionists vote Labour.'

Such a law is restricted in scope, not only by virtue of referring to a social category (trade unionists) that is found in only a restricted range of societies, but even more decisively through its reference to named *individuals* – in this case to contemporary Britain (an individual country) and the British Labour Party (an individual organization).

Some writers deny that social science is peculiar in this latter respect. In illustration they often cite Kepler's Laws, which describe the paths of planets *in the solar system*, thereby referring to a named individual entity, the sun. But there is a crucial difference. The motions of planets round the sun come within the scope of a highly general universal law, the Law of Gravitation (which in fact predicts them slightly more accurately than do Kepler's Laws). Similarly, while physical laws can also be restricted in scope in the sense of holding only in certain circumstances, both their holding in these circumstances and their failure to hold in others are often explicable by more general laws. Thus Newtonian mechanics (apparently) holds good except in relation to very small and very fast-moving entities; this is explained by the highly general laws of relativity and quantum theory. The restricted laws of social science can rarely be replaced or explained by more general laws.

Like precision and generality, and like generality and universality, universality and precision are often alternative virtues between which the social scientist must choose. We have seen that many social science laws are not too clear in meaning. They can perhaps be made clear; but there is then a choice as to how specifically to formulate them. Take law (6): the vague term 'stratified society' could be taken to refer to *any* inequality of wealth or status, however slight; or (at the other extreme) only to a high degree of inequality. On the former interpretation the law may well be truly universal but it is extremely unspecific (and trivial); on the latter, it is much more specific but will certainly be less universally true.[9]

Unlike universal laws, probabilistic laws do not imply firm predictions about particular cases. The predictions they allow are not only merely probabilistic, in addition the prediction that a certain outcome is probable has only a limited validity, as the following example (adapted from Quentin Gibson)[10] shows. It is apparently true that in contemporary Britain most trade unionists vote Labour. But it does not follow that if a man is a trade unionist he probably votes Labour. Perhaps his father voted Conservative, and perhaps most people vote as their father voted (another probabilistic law). If so, we seem to need a law about the voting behaviour of trade unionists whose fathers voted Conservative. But even if known, such a law, so long as it is only probabilistic, may always omit some *further* factor which affects the probabilities. The best we can say is that, *relative to our knowledge of the facts of the case and of their relevance*, a certain outcome seems probable.

Before leaving the subject of non-universal laws, we should consider a further form these can take, namely so-called *tendency laws* (for example: 'Women *tend* to vote for right-wing parties'). This is a rather ambiguous expression. It might, for example, be just an alternative name for a probabilistic law. On the other hand, Quentin Gibson defines a 'tendency statement'[11] as a law stating what always happens unless 'interfering' conditions prevent it; thus, the example above would mean that women vote for right-wing parties in the absence of interfering conditions. Unfortunately, this is compatible with women *never* voting for right-wing parties, which suggests that Gibson's interpretation is unhelpful. Indeed, it allows one to call anything whatever a tendency, for of anything whatever it can be said that it always happens if interfering conditions do not prevent it. A more useful interpretation is in terms of *relative proportions*. Our example would then mean that a *higher proportion* of women than of men vote for right-wing parties. In general terms: 'As *tend* to be Bs' is equivalent to 'A higher proportion of As than of non-As are Bs'. Social science laws often take this form, which expresses essentially the same idea as that of a *correlation* between A and B. The predictive utility of such a correlational law (or tendency law) is limited. It tells one nothing about the probability that an A or a non-A is a B, except that, in the relative sense explained above, the former is greater than the latter. If it is true that women tend to vote for right-wing parties, right-wing parties wishing to increase their share of the vote should (other things being equal) support the enfranchisement of women; but whether this is likely to turn defeats into victories (rather than make their defeats narrower or their victories more comfortable) the tendency law cannot tell us.

The search for correlations plays a large role in social science, and a separate section will be devoted to the topic at the end of this chapter.

[10] Cf. Q. Gibson, *op. cit.*, pp. 126–30. Gibson takes a rather different position on the issue, however.
[11] *Ibid.*, p. 18.

But meanwhile we must consider a further alleged defect of social science laws, namely their *untheoretical* nature. Usually (especially in the case of correlational laws) they are derived inductively from regularities found in experimental data and, unlike comparable regularity statements in physics, are not derivable from theoretical laws. The lack of theoretical laws in social science is connected with the low generality of its laws, for the theoretical laws of physics are more general than the empirical regularities – they serve to explain and hence unify a rather wide range of the latter (we saw that the various regularities involved in the melting of solids are explained by theoretical laws relating to bonds between molecules). A physical theory thus amounts to a *system* of deductively connected laws, theoretical and empirical. Only in economics among the social sciences is there a unified systematic theory at all comparable with those of physics.

Ernest Nagel has suggested[12] that there is also a connection between the lack of theory in social science, and the lack of precision and universality of its laws. He points out that, while there is a precise law of physics of universal form, asserting that the distance that a body falls from rest is proportional to the square of the time of fall, this law would not in fact appear to be supported by observations of different sorts of bodies falling in various conditions. Such observations would show only a *positive correlation* between distance and time – that is, of two falling bodies the one that fell longer would usually fall further, but not always. For the law applies only to a simplified 'ideal model', that of a body falling in a perfect vacuum – a phenomenon never observed. We saw[13] that from such theoretical laws can be derived empirical laws that apply to the real world – empirical laws that are unified into a system by their common derivation. According to Nagel, it is because the social sciences rarely adopt this strategy, but instead try to work out laws from knowledge of particular facts, that their laws are not universal or precise. Sometimes, admittedly, they do adopt such a strategy – for example in economics, which from simplified assumptions has derived a large body of systematic theoretical laws. But here, unlike in physics, there is uncertainty as to how to relate these laws to reality.

This brings us to the most severe defect from which social science laws in general suffer – their uncertain relation to reality. This is apparent from the list cited earlier, for laws (4) and (5), for example, are contradictory – yet both are believed. If (5) is understood probabilistically, the contradiction disappears – (4) and (3) could then be taken as together specifying more precisely the scope of (5). But whether this set of laws (3), (4) and (5) is warranted by the facts is another matter.

---

[12] In *op. cit.*, pp. 508–9.   [13] Above, pp. 28–9.

Indeed, just what social laws the facts do support is very much subject to dispute.

Let us now move on from listing the deficiencies of social science laws to deeper questions. Are these deficiencies due to the intrinsic nature of the subject matter, or to various 'accidental' handicaps (such as the difficulties of experimentation in social science)? How, if at all, might the social sciences achieve precise, highly general universal laws, integrated into a system of theory and well corroborated by known facts? Nagel seems to imply that the best hope is to develop the implications of simplified 'ideal models' and this is reminiscent of a celebrated methodological prescription of Max Weber, namely the method of *ideal types* (conceived of by Weber, however, as peculiar to the 'cultural' – i.e. social – sciences). This methodology of Weber's is sufficiently complex and important to merit extended consideration.[14]

Ideal types

Weber notoriously used the expression 'ideal type' in various different and overlapping ways. In order to elucidate it, let us start from the fact that in societies of different times and places one can recognize institutions which, while organized in diverse ways, are functionally similar – there are diverse economic institutions (institutions by means of which goods and services are produced and distributed), diverse political, religious, etc., institutions. Within the group of (say) economic institutions there are both similarities and differences. We can, Weber held, best order this variety intellectually by an abstraction from historical reality. The various forms express, to a greater or lesser degree, different *principles* for the conduct of economic (or political, etc.) life: the task of analysis is to abstract these principles in a pure (or 'ideal') form, and use them to construct 'ideal types'. The latter represent contrasting possibilities in the organization of economic (or political, etc.) life, based on historical reality but not simply a description of it, for they embody a 'one-sided accentuation' of certain of its features. In economics, Weber mentions the following ideal types: the 'city economy' (dominant in late medieval Europe); 'handicraft production'; and 'capitalism' (which would be defined in terms of private ownership of the means of production, production by legally free wage-labour, distribution by buying and selling on a free competitive market, etc.); while in politics Weber treats at some length the three famous ideal types of authority – legal, traditional, and charismatic.[15]

[14] For Weber on ideal types, see his *The Methodology of the Social Sciences* (Glencoe, Free Press, 1949), pp. 42–4, 89–106; also his *The Theory of Social and Economic Organization*, pp. 92, 110–12.

[15] For the economic ideal types, see *The Methodology of the Social Sciences*, pp. 90–1; for the political, *The Theory of Social and Economic Organization*, pp. 324–92.

These ideal types are not classificatory categories under which individual phenomena are subsumable, but 'extreme' forms which individual phenomena resemble to a greater or lesser degree. Hence, as Dennis Wrong has complained,[16] they cannot be the subjects of empirical laws. But they have other uses. They still have a classificatory function, in that historically real institutions can be described in terms of their similarity to and divergence from the ideal types, as mixtures of elements of different ideal types, etc. This of course presupposes some description of the individual historical phenomena, and here again Weber recommends the ideal type method: that is, a 'historical individual' such as Calvinism, the Prussian state, or the economy of Western Europe in a particular period, should be reduced to its leading principles by a 'purifying' abstraction from the relatively confused and complex reality. The ideal type of the historical individual can then be compared with the relevant range of 'classificatory' ideal types.

The latter have a second use more germane to our present theme: they can (sometimes) be used in constructing the sort of 'ideal model' that Nagel sees as a suitable device for generating scientific theories. Thus, assuming that the people involved in economic life act within a framework of ideal typical 'capitalist' institutions, and also *pursue certain goals in a completely 'rational' way within the restraints inherent in these institutions*, it is possible to work out relationships between supply, demand, price, savings, investment, etc. The propositions expressing these relationships constitute an economic theory. Weber suggests that classical and neo-classical economic theory was worked out in precisely this way (perhaps not consciously), on the assumption that economic actors rationally pursue maximum income.[17] Rather confusingly, Weber calls such a theory, too, an ideal type.

This 'theoretical' ideal type involves *three* levels of abstraction (i.e. unreality). Firstly, the institutional reality seldom corresponds perfectly to the (classificatory) ideal type of capitalism (some means of production may be publicly owned, free competition may be somewhat restricted, etc.); secondly, people's motives will in reality be more complex than the imputed desire to maximize income; thirdly, there will be many departures from perfect rationality in the pursuit of goals – due to ignorance, errors, miscalculations, etc. Hence the ideal typical theory will by no means be a perfectly accurate description of economic reality. How, then, is it to be related to reality? (This is the problem Nagel raises.) Weber's answer appears to be two-fold. Firstly, the assumptions of the ideal type, if well chosen, should be such that its divergences from reality are in many cases not great. Secondly, in so far as an ideal typical theory diverges from reality in a particular case, this alerts the

---

[16] In his *Max Weber* (Englewood Cliffs, Prentice-Hall, 1970), p. 154.

[17] See *The Methodology of the Social Sciences*, pp. 43–4, 89–90.

investigator to look for those respects in which its assumptions are inaccurate in that case.[18] For example, in so far as an approximately capitalist economy diverges from the predictions of economic theory, one should seek an explanation in such 'distorting' factors as (say) public monopolies, non-economic motives, or irrationalities. The ideal type analysis facilitates identification of *departures* from the ideal type and their significance.

Because of the institutional assumptions built into a theoretical ideal type, it might seem that a social science theory constructed on Weberian lines must be of relatively limited applicability. Economic theory, for example, is apparently restricted in application to societies whose economic institutions do not greatly depart from ideal typical 'capitalism'. But this is not *necessarily* so. One *might* apply similar assumptions about motives and rationality to different institutional settings, and thus derive bodies of economic laws applicable to them. *All* the laws derived from given assumptions about motives would then form parts of a single economic theory. But since for Weber a social science theory depends on specific and simplified assumptions as to motive and rationality, it is unlikely ever to be a completely accurate description of reality, though it can come close to it when the assumptions are not too unrealistic. In some cases, however, the unreality could be extreme. Let us now raise the question whether this conception of social theory, including particularly economic theory, is correct.

Economic theory
According to Lionel Robbins, such a conception of economic theory is incorrect.[19] Robbins denies that economic theory is premised on particular motives: it assumes only that people have *scales of relative valuation* – i.e. value different states of affairs unequally – which is a psychological truism universally applicable. Consider the law that under free market conditions payment of a bounty (subsidy) for the production of a commodity increases production of that commodity. This law does not, as might be thought, depend on the assumption that producers seek solely to maximize money gains – only that money can be of some use to them in bringing about a more valued state of affairs. They may, of course, value some things that money cannot buy (the esteem of their neighbours, etc.), but so long as *something* they value is purchasable, it is rational for them to produce more of a commodity subsidized than unsubsidized. Robbins assumes that, given a free market, this is always the case. However, as Robbins would agree, without knowing the exact relative valuations of the producers it is not possible to state

[18] See *The Methodology of the Social Sciences*, pp. 101–2.
[19] See his *The Nature and Significance of Economic Science*, 2nd edn (London, Macmillan, 1948), pp. 75–86, 90–9.

an *exact quantitative relation* between the amount of bounty and the increase in production. He points out[20] that because people's valuations differ in different times and places, economic laws will be *unspecific*: but, contrary to Weber, differing valuations do not make economic laws in varying degrees *inaccurate*.

Robbins argues further that economic theory, again contrary to Weber, is perfectly general in application, that is, not limited to particular societies. True, the law quoted above is stated by Robbins to be, like many economic laws, applicable only to free market conditions (not, for example, to the planned economies of the so-called 'communist' countries, where the government seeks to determine output levels by decree). But Robbins would argue that these laws are merely relatively particular applications of more general principles. Although he does not state the general principle of which the above law is a particularization, it is implied by another principle which is, he says,[21] basic in the theory of labour distribution: 'Workers seek to maximize their net advantages from work'. The corresponding basic principle in the theory of production would be: 'Producers seek to maximize their net advantages from production'. Certainly this principle appears to be applicable to producers in any sort of economic system, and to explain the free-market law we have been discussing.

Nevertheless, I believe that Robbins's account of economic theory is mistaken on some points where it contradicts Weber's. Firstly, he is wrong to assert that, given free competitive markets, a bounty will *always* increase production. It is true that the bounty increases the producer's profit per unit of output. But we *cannot* assume (as Robbins does) that producers will be able to buy something they want with the increased money income they would get by producing more – they may already be able to buy all they want that is purchasable. In our culture, we are accustomed to suppose that however much people can buy, they will always want to buy more. Robbins supposes this to be a universal attitude, but it is not. In 'traditionalist' societies – societies where consumption levels are fixed by traditional norms – the amount of money income desired may be quite low. It is then perfectly possible that a bounty will *reduce* production, for it will reduce the number of units that a man has to produce and sell in order to attain the traditionally determined income. To consume purchasable commodities in excess of this level, perhaps, would arouse the hostility of neighbours. If producers value the esteem of neighbours, leisure, etc., more highly than extra purchasable commodities, it will be rational for them to react to a bounty by producing less, for this is the way to 'maximize their net

[20] See *The Nature and Significance of Economic Science*, 2nd edn pp. 106–12.
[21] *Ibid.*, pp. 95–6.

advantages'. Analogously, workers in a traditionalist society react to an increase in wages by working less, not more – as experience (notwithstanding economic theory) has repeatedly shown, and as Weber knew.[22]

The implication of this is that Robbins's completely general economic principles are, if completely general, tautological (in Popperian language, unfalsifiable); or, if non-tautological, *not* really general but 'culture-bound'. The principle that 'workers (producers) seek to maximize their net advantages from work (production)' is generally true only in the sense that *whatever* workers (etc.) do *must* be what they think maximizes their net advantages. In that sense it tells us no more than that workers (etc.) do whatever they do. The principle can be made non-tautological only by *specifying* what workers (etc.) see as 'advantages'. We have seen that orthodox economic theory did implicitly specify this in a particular way, and thus produced laws which hold in some cultures but not in others.

This neglect of cultural differences explains why orthodox economic theory is of so little use in relation to 'developing' countries. These are transitional rather than traditionalist societies, and it is not so much desire for increased money income that is lacking, as other attitudes assumed by orthodox economics. Take, for example, the theory of investment (a matter crucial to economic development), according to which the availability of high profits from the production of a commodity leads to substantial investment in that line of production. But investment requires other values besides a desire for more money. It requires willingness to take risks (especially if the investment has a long gestation period), for miscalculation or unforeseen change may turn the expected profit into a loss; and it requires abstinence from current consumption – saving. In mature capitalist cultures, risk-taking and abstinence are admired as virtues (and called respectively 'enterprise' and 'thrift'), but these attitudes are not universal. In traditional and transitional societies, therefore, people may (perfectly rationally) prefer 'conspicuous consumption' to saving and investment, or may prefer to invest in safe (and socially prestigious) assets such as land, rather than in risky (even if possibly profitable) production; and in that case, the investment that orthodox economics predicts does not occur, or occurs to an insignificant degree. Another possible reason for this may be a paucity of investment-facilitating *institutions* in such societies. (This whole situation helps to explain why governments often play a prominent role in investment in developing countries).

According to Robbins, economic laws do not presuppose particular scales of evaluation because they are not very precise. Some economic laws, however, *are* precise and therefore *do* presuppose single-minded

[22] Cf. M. Weber, *The Protestant Ethic and the Spirit of Capitalism* (London, Allen and Unwin, 1930), pp. 58–60.

REGULARITIES IN SOCIAL SCIENCE 63

maximization of a specific value – or else they are tautological. The first of our earlier list of social science laws is an example. This law presupposes conditions of 'perfect competition', a concept which includes some of the prerequisites of perfectly rational pursuit of goals, such as perfect information. But even given this, the law will hold only if firms seek solely to maximize money profit. The law derives from the premise that producers will produce a given unit of output if, and only if, the price received for it is at least equal to the cost of producing it. If, however, producers value (positively or negatively) non-monetary consequences of production (if they take pride in workmanship or resent loss of leisure, for example), the premise, and the law, are unwarranted. At least, this is so if the word 'cost' is interpreted in purely monetary terms; and admittedly it *can* be understood in such a way as to include non-monetary 'costs' such as loss of leisure. But only if 'cost' were understood as a sum embracing all these non-monetary elements – including non-monetary *benefits* as negative costs – would what the law asserts be true, and it would then be tautological in the sense already discussed. Only if 'cost' is understood as money cost, and producers value nothing about production but money costs and receipts, does the assertion hold as an exact quantitative law. The latter condition is unlikely to be fulfilled even in cultures where money costs and receipts bulk large in people's plans. Thus the exact quantitative law is never likely to be completely accurate, though in appropriate cultures it will not be too far out. This accords with Weber's conception of ideal typical theory.

As a matter of fact, even if the people involved in economic production were interested only in maximizing money gains, it does not necessarily follow that firms in a capitalist market system would aim solely to maximize money profit. This is the implication of J. K. Galbraith's well-known thesis about the large modern corporation.[23] These firms, he asserts, have become less interested in profit and increasingly concerned with other goals, such as security and growth – not because producers are less interested in money gains, but because *power* has passed from entrepreneurs to salaried managers and technical experts whose money income is relatively independent of their firm's profit. In other words, the structure of producing units – an institutional matter – affects their 'goals'. Galbraith's thesis implies that our exact economic law is a decreasingly accurate description of capitalist economies.

Our discussion of economic theory can be summarized as follows. *All* non-tautological economic laws are culture-bound (that is, valid only given appropriate values). *Exact* economic laws are practically

[23] See his *The New Industrial State* (London, Hamish Hamilton, 1967), esp. ch. 15.

never perfectly accurate, but in appropriate cultures are not too inaccurate. *Inexact* laws may hold in some cultures, but not in others.

Social science theory in general

What light does our discussion of economic theory throw on social science theory in general ? Economics is in important ways untypical, notably in the ready quantifiability of its concepts (price, cost, output, etc.) – this is one reason why theory in other social sciences is much less developed. But all social science theories do appear to depend on assumptions about values, attitudes, etc. These must either vary from culture to culture or be the same in all cultures (i.e. part of 'human nature'). To what extent is there a general human nature ?

George Homans has argued,[24] in effect, that there *is* a general human nature, described by *psychological* laws, which must form the basis of all social science. From these basic psychological laws (such as 'the higher the value a person sets [on the expected result of an action], the more likely he is to take the action') one can, says Homans, derive the laws of economics, including *both* the law that high price reduces demand *and* the opposite law of 'conspicuous consumption', that high price increases demand (both follow from the psychological law quoted above – the latter applies when a people set a high value on spending conspicuously); also the laws of *conformity* (to social institutions), of *deviance*, and of *institutional change* (people conform when conformity is more valued than deviance, and vice-versa – if enough are deviant, institutions change); and indeed all social laws whatever.

The trouble with this is that Homans's basic psychological law (quoted above) is extremely reminiscent of the proposition (discussed earlier) that economic actors seek to maximize net advantage. It is, in other words, tautological. Nothing in particular can be derived from it unless one specifies what a person values. Any social law derived in this way must be culture-bound unless the evaluations on which it depends are completely general *human* evaluations.

Doubtless there are some universal human attitudes, but it is easy to overestimate their number. Classical and neo-classical economic theorists seem to have made precisely the mistake (dubbed 'reification' by Marx) of supposing that the attitudes of a particular culture were part of human nature itself. The belief in certain completely general, universal social laws may rest on a similar mistake. Thus, the law that 'all societies are stratified' is often based on a 'functionalist' theoretical premise to the effect that people will not be willing to carry out onerous tasks without special rewards.[25] Again, the law that 'all societies are

---

[24] See his *The Nature of Social Science*, pp. 35–58.
[25] See, for example, K. Davis and W. E. Moore, 'Some Principles of Stratification', *American Sociological Review*, vol. 10 (1945), pp. 242–4.

ruled by an oligarchy', associated with Robert Michels,[26] rests on a complex theoretical analysis, a crucial part of which is that in all societies most people would rather be ruled than rule themselves. Whether these premises about human nature are universally true is of the greatest importance, for on their *not* being universally true depends the possibility of equality and democracy. If human nature is less uniform than these theories suppose – if equality and democracy are possible even if rare – then the two laws can of course only be probabilistic, not universal. It could, indeed, be argued that, notwithstanding Michels, democracy (or at least non-oligarchy) actually exists in some modern societies, partly due to attitudes different from those he assumes.

We have by now seen good reasons why social science laws should so often suffer from defects mentioned earlier in the chapter – lack of specificity, of generality, and of universality. They are consequences above all of the variability of human motives, attitudes, and evaluations. Nor are these defects likely to be cured, as Nagel suggests,[27] by following the 'ideal model' or 'ideal type' strategy. Economic theory, for example, which follows that strategy, produces, for the most part, unspecific laws of fairly narrow applicability. The difference between physical and social science here is that social science theory is affected by what might be called *quasi free will*. The human will may or may not be free, in an ultimate sense; that is, it may or may not be the case that people's motives, attitudes and values at every moment are determined and in principle predictable. In practice, however, they cannot be predicted. Hence social science theory, as we have seen, makes simplified assumptions about typical motives, etc. So far as a particular individual is concerned, these assumptions may be completely unrealistic. But since social science laws do not aim to describe the behaviour of individuals as such, but of groups, it suffices if the assumed motivations are widespread in these groups. More precisely, it suffices for relatively unspecific laws – exact quantitative laws (relating, say, production bounties to changes in output) would require that the reaction of each individual to given circumstances be predictable. And it is because human motivations are in fact variable but have to be taken as given for the purposes of social science theory that its laws have a relatively narrow scope and do not hold universally. Social science laws have the characteristics that would be the consequence of human free will, if it existed.

How serious are the defects of social science laws from the point of view of their 'scientific' status? Popper's criterion for the scientificity of a law-statement, it will be remembered, is that it should be in

---

[26] See his *Political Parties* (New York, Dover, 1959), esp. Part One, chs V and VII, and Part Six, chs II and IV.

[27] See above, pp. 57–8.

E

principle falsifiable by statements based on observation describing particular facts.[28] (In social science, we have argued, descriptions of particular facts require that observation be interpreted in terms of mentalistic categories, but that makes no essential difference). From this point of view it is obvious that lack of *clarity* is a grave defect, for it makes it uncertain whether a particular fact is or is not consistent with a supposed law. Deliberate vagueness can indeed be used precisely to make falsification difficult, and no doubt often has been by social theorists. But there is no reason why descriptive social concepts *have* to be unclear, and most social scientists realize that scientific concepts need to be clearly defined. Lack of *specificity* and *generality* are, from a Popperian point of view, regrettable but not disastrous – each reduces the number of a law's 'potential falsifiers' and so makes it *a priori* less vulnerable, but not invulnerable, to falsification.

What about lack of *universality*? We saw in the first chapter[29] that the non-universal form of quantum physical laws raises special problems. These can be (more or less) solved because the laws are very precise and refer to microscopic processes, very large numbers of which correspond to observable macro-phenomena. But the social sciences' non-universal (probabilistic) laws can never be numerically precise, and refer to macro-phenomena directly. How can such a law as 'The great majority of societies are ruled by an oligarchy' be falsified, bearing in mind the imprecision of the expression 'the great majority' and the fact that the law refers to the great majority of *all* societies, past, present, and future?

Actually, the situation is not as desperate as this may suggest. It is a mistake to assimilate probabilistic laws too closely to the statistical laws of quantum physics. Although they share the statistical form 'x% of As are Bs', in quantum physics the aim is to specify x as *precisely* as possible – there is no merit in x being high – whereas in a probabilistic law x should be as *high* as possible. Probabilistic laws, unlike the statistical quantum laws, are, so to speak, *attempts at universal laws* – the nearest to universal laws that the subject-matter allows. All that is required, then, is that social science laws be such that they *would* be falsifiable if stated in universal form. They can then be compared with the facts to see to what extent they are corroborated and discorroborated, exactly as if they *were* universal in form. A probabilistic law can be considered a universal law to which exceptions – falsifying instances – are bound to exist. The fewer the better, of course – that is, the more corroborating instances and the fewer discorroborating instances, the better. Or, one might say, the *more nearly universally* a law appears to hold, on the evidence, the better – other things equal. For universality

---

[28] See above, p. 18. [29] Above, pp. 19–21.

is of course not the only virtue of laws – generality and specificity are virtues too, and as we saw above, virtues which may conflict with universality.

Practical difficulties in testing social science laws

It is not enough that laws should be in principle testable, they must also be tested. Here social science suffers from a well-known and serious difficulty: it is usually impossible (for practical and moral reasons) to test social science laws by *controlled experiment*. More precisely, this is a serious difficulty in relation to *causal laws* – that is, laws which assert a relation of succession between kinds of events, such as the law that a bounty increases output. Non-causal laws, for example the law that all societies are stratified, are testable without controlled experiments; this law is testable by studying societies just as they happen to be. But causal laws usually have to be understood as subject to the famous qualifying phrase, 'other things remaining equal'. Thus, the introduction of a bounty may not increase output if other things change – if, for example, there is simultaneously a decline in demand for the commodity in question. The law really states that a bounty makes output higher *than it otherwise would be*. Strictly, one can never know what would have happened in such a non-existent situation, but in physical science the function of the controlled experiment is to permit comparison of two situations in which 'other things' *are* equal; to enable the scientist to vary a single factor at a time so as to test whether this change produces the result that theory predicts. It is obviously not possible to introduce a bounty in such a controlled situation, except perhaps in a completely totalitarian society. Thus, the corroboratory or discorroboratory significance of social experience in relation to social science laws is often quite doubtful. This is one potent reason why, as mentioned earlier, the relation of these laws to reality is frequently uncertain and subject to dispute.

In a situation in which various factors influence an outcome in an uncontrolled way, one expedient is to resort to *statistical analysis* of large numbers of cases; that is, to look for *correlations* between variables. This search is so pervasive in social science that it deserves consideration at some length.

Correlation[30]

Let us begin by distinguishing three sorts of data: nominal, ordinal and cardinal. *Nominal* data are data which are categorized but not quantified; for example, people may be categorized as men or women, Protestants

[30] In writing this and the following section I have been greatly helped by discussions with Professor S. D. Silvey, Mr Peter Norman, and Professor A. M. Potter.

or Catholics, working-class or middle-class. *Ordinal* data are quantified to the extent that individuals can be put in a rank order for some variable, but are not assigned a numerical value; for example, we may be able to order individuals from those with most prestige to those with least, without being able to measure each person's prestige numerically. *Cardinal* data are numerically quantified; we can, for example, describe people's income in terms of a numerical measure.

The idea of correlation is applicable to all these three kinds of data, as is that of a universal law. 'All As are Bs' is a universal law about nominal data. If to this law we add another, 'All non-As are non-Bs' (equivalent to 'All Bs are As'), the two together are equivalent to a *perfect positive correlation* between A and B. (Perfect correlation is essentially similar to Hume's constant conjunction). But correlation is a matter of degree; if a higher proportion of As than of non-As are Bs, there is a positive correlation between A and B, though not a perfect one. Thus, if a higher proportion of women than of men vote for right-wing parties, there is a positive correlation between female sex and right-wing voting, and a negative correlation between male sex and right-wing voting. If the proportions are equal, the correlation between sex and right-wing voting is zero.

As for ordinal data, perfect positive correlation is expressed by a universal law of the form 'The higher A is, the higher B is'; perfect negative correlation by a law of the form 'The higher A is, the lower B is'. For example, there might conceivably be a perfect positive (ordinal) correlation between prestige and income; if so, whenever we compare two individuals we will always find that the one with the higher income has the higher prestige, and vice-versa (and similarly *mutatis mutandis* if we compare one individual at two different times). Again, correlation can be imperfect without being zero. If it is positive but not perfect, the proportion of pair-wise comparisons in which higher income is associated with higher prestige is greater than the proportion in which higher income is associated with lower prestige; if the two proportions are the same, the correlation is zero.

To explain correlations of cardinal data it is necessary to draw a graph. In Figure 1, the line AB represents the quantity y as a linear function of x. It has the general formula

$$y = a + bx$$

where a represents the distance OA (the value of y when x is zero) and b represents the steepness of slope of AB. Such a line as AB is equivalent to an *exact quantitative universal law* stating a functional relation between two variables, like the law that the distance a body falls in a given time is proportional to the square of the time (in this case y would represent distance and x the square of the time, and a would be zero – that is, A and O coincide). It also represents a perfect correlation between the two variables. But once again correlation may be less than perfect though not zero. If, say, years of education and income are positively but not perfectly correlated, then, plotting years of education (x) against income (y) we will find that not all points on the graph

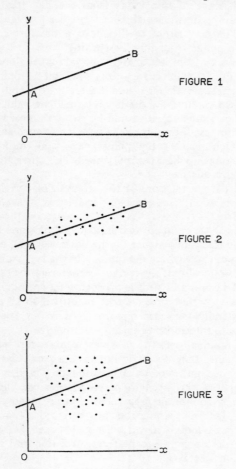

FIGURE 1

FIGURE 2

FIGURE 3

lie on a straight line like AB, but they do show a tendency to *cluster* round such a line, as in Figure 2, rather than to be scattered at random, as in Figure 3.

For each of the three sorts of data, it is possible to calculate the *strength* of correlation manifested by any set of data. For cardinal data, strength (and direction) of correlation are measured by the *correlation coefficient* (r) which varies from -1 to $+1$. Its meaning is roughly as follows. For any set of measurements of two variables (such as income and years of education) points can be plotted on a graph as in Figure 2. It is then possible to draw a straight line (such as AB) which minimizes the average distance of the points from the line (that is, no other straight line can be drawn which is at a smaller average distance from the points). The correlation coefficient is a measure of the average distance of the points from this 'best-fitting' line. It is positive if the line slopes upwards from left to right, negative if it slopes downwards from left to right. Its value is 1 ($+1$ or -1) if all the points fall exactly on the line (perfect correlation), zero if there is no correlation whatever between the two variables, and takes intermediate values accordingly. (The correlation coefficient, it should be stressed, measures only *linear* correlation. The best-fitting line may be a curve such as a parabola or hyperbola, which may fit the points very well, indicating a close functional relationship between variables. The correlation coefficient does not measure this.)

For ordinal data, a measure of the strength of correlation (that is, rank-order correlation) between two variables is *Kendall's tau*, which again varies from -1 to $+1$. Its value depends on the proportion of cases in which, if we compare two individuals, the one ranked higher on one variable also ranks higher on the other variable, compared with the proportion of cases where the ranking of the two individuals on the two variables is opposite. If the two proportions are the same, Kendall's tau is zero; if in all cases the rank orders of two individuals are the same, tau is $+1$ (perfect positive correlation); if in all cases the rank orders of two individuals are opposite, tau is -1 (perfect negative correlation); with intermediate values accordingly.

Finally, for nominal data where we are comparing two categories in relation to whether they do or do not have a particular characteristic (for example, men and women in relation to whether they vote for right-wing parties), the strength of correlation can be expressed in terms of the *difference in the proportions* of each category that have the characteristic. If each proportion is expressed as a fraction, the difference between them will vary, again, between -1 and $+1$, with the extremes corresponding to perfect correlation and the value zero to no correlation whatever.

It is also possible to work out a correlation coefficient (r) in relation to nominal data which is in *aggregative* form. We may for example, be interested in a possible correlation between social class and voting behaviour, and have data on voting patterns and numbers of class members in the various constituencies of a country. This data about constituencies aggregates *nominal* data about individuals – their class and voting behaviour – into *numerical* form, thus permitting calculation of the correlation coefficient relating, say, proportion of right-wing voters and proportion of non-working class voters in these constituencies. But the coefficient is not strictly a measure of the correlation between being non-working class and voting for a right-wing party. For suppose the measured correlation coefficient is positive and high: it is possible in principle, so far as the statistics go – however unlikely intuitively – that the reason is not that non-working class people tend to vote for right-wing parties, but that the higher the proportion of non-working class people in a constituency the more the *working class* tends to vote for right-wing parties, while other classes on average favour right-wing parties no more than does the working-class.

What is the relation between measures of correlation and the testing of laws ? We have seen that perfect correlation always corresponds to universal laws (in the case of nominal data, to two universal laws); that is, if certain laws hold universally, the corresponding correlations will always be perfect. A measure of correlation is always, of course, relative to a particular set of data, and it is in fact a measure of the degree to which that set of data corroborates (or conforms to) the law or laws corresponding to perfect correlation. Thus, the law 'The higher a person's income, the greater his prestige' is corroborated as much as it could be by a particular set of data if those data yield a value of Kendall's tau $= + 1$ for correlation of income and prestige; it is discorroborated as much as it could be if Kendall's tau $= - 1$ for this correlation; and correspondingly for intermediate values. A similar interpretation holds for the other correlation measures. But where the correlation coefficient is involved, the law in question is of course an exact quantitative law defined by the 'best-fitting line'; and the measure of correlation for nominal data defined above measures simultaneously the conformity of the data to *two* laws (of the form 'All As are Bs' and 'All non-As are non-Bs'. If all As in a set of data were Bs, the measured correlation of A and B would still be zero if all non-As in the data were also Bs). Thus, correlational laws are like probabilistic laws: they are not themselves falsifiable, but are testable through the falsifiability of corresponding universal laws.

Sampling and significance

Social scientists, when they compute a measure of correlation for given data, often go on to work out the so-called *significance level* of the computed value. Thus, a computed correlation coefficient for education and income may be said to be significant, or not significant, at the 5% level, etc. It is important to realize that this 'significance' tells one nothing whatever about the correlation of education and income among people in general. It has meaning only if the data for which the correlation coefficient was calculated constitute a *random sample* of a specific population (say, British adults in 1972), and it gives some information about the probability that a correlation exists *in that population*. The only relevance, therefore, of 'significance level' to the testing of universal laws is that it provides some indirect and inconclusive evidence of the degree to which that population corroborates and discorroborates such a law.

Suppose the correlation coefficient (r) relating education and income in a random sample of size n drawn from same population is $+0 \cdot 6$ (a random sample is one in which each individual in the population has an equal chance of inclusion, and so has each combination of individuals). Although $r = +0 \cdot 6$, the correlation coefficient for education and income in the *population* (ρ) might, if we could compute it, be found to have any of a wide range of values, positive, negative, or zero. By hypothesis, however, we cannot compute ρ. Now, if in fact $\rho = 0$, and repeated independent random samples of size n are drawn from the population and the value of r is computed for each sample, the values of r assume in the long run a specific frequency distribution (the most frequent values are naturally at and near zero, the least frequent nearest to $+1$ and -1). One can thus say, for example, in what proportion of such samples from a population in which $\rho = 0$, r is $+0 \cdot 6$ *or greater*. Suppose the proportion is 5%. Statisticians will then say that our computed r of $+0 \cdot 6$ is significant at the 5% level. What does this mean?

When we sample populations in which $\rho = 0$, 5% of samples show *positive* correlations significant at the 5% level. When we sample populations in which ρ is *negative, fewer* than 5% of samples show *positive* correlations significant at the 5% level. Suppose we adopt this rule: if we find a sample correlation positive and significant at the 5% level or better, we will infer that there is a positive correlation in the population from which the sample was drawn. Otherwise we infer nothing. Now, if all our samples came from populations in which ρ is zero or negative, all these inferences would be wrong, but we would not make these erroneous inferences in more than 5% of the cases. Since in fact some populations have positive correlations, the general application of our rule will mean that some of our inferences are right, though we cannot say how many – all we can say is that the number of erroneous inferences, as a proportion of all cases (*not* of all inferences) will not, in the long run, exceed 5%. This is the meaning of the expression that a given sample correlation coefficient is significant at the 5% level.

It is to be noticed what a very limited meaning this expression has. If we *apply* our rule of inference (together with a corresponding rule when r is negative) on x occasions, actually *infer* that ρ is positive or that it is negative on y occasions, and so infer *erroneously* on z occasions, then the proportion $\frac{z}{x}$ will not exceed 5% in the long run (it would be 5% if all ρ's were zero, and less than 5% otherwise). That is all. We know nothing about $\frac{z}{y}$ or $\frac{y-z}{y}$ (the proportion of inferences that are correct). This remains true whatever the significance level used in the inference rule – whether it is 5%, 1% or 0·001%. What is more, even this limited claim to knowledge depends, in the case of correlation coefficients, on the assumption that the correlated variables are *normally distributed* in the population, with extreme values having the lowest frequencies and opposite extremes equal frequencies. This assumption does not hold, for example, in relation to income in most communities, where the poor are much more numerous than the rich. In such a case one might prefer to use Kendall's tau, the rank-order correlation measure, for which significance level can be calculated in the same way as for the correlation coefficient, but without requiring the assumption of normal distribution. It is also possible to attach a significance level to a sample correlation measured on nominal data.

In addition, the inference involved – that two variables are positively correlated or are negatively correlated in a given population – besides having a highly indirect and uncertain justification, is an extremely unspecific one. Nothing about the degree of (positive or negative) correlation in a population can be inferred from the significance level of a sample correlation. Hence, even if the inference is correct, it does not indicate very precisely the degree to which the population corroborates or discorroborates the universal law or laws corresponding to perfect correlation. However, it is possible – and a good deal more useful – to compute a *confidence interval* in relation to a measured correlation for a sample of a given size. Suppose that in some random sample the measured correlation of two variables is +0·6. Then one can calculate, say, a 95% confidence interval, which is a range of values that includes +0·6 (say, +0·5 to +0·68). There is then a 95% probability that the population correlation lies within this range (that is, the inference that the population correlation lies within a range calculated in this way is correct on 95% of occasions). The probability can be made higher by calculating, say, a 99% confidence interval. But the higher the confidence, the larger the interval.

Confidence intervals are much more informative than significance levels, but even they are informative only about a specific population from which a random sample has been drawn. Correlations that hold in one such population need not hold in another, even if the latter is a sub-population of the former. (If there was a positive correlation between female sex and right-wing voting in the British general election of 1970, it does not follow that there was such a correlation among

Scottish voters, or middle-class voters, in the 1970 election). The variability of human values and attitudes makes such differences between populations and sub-populations quite likely.

Finally, a word on so-called 'spurious correlations'. A positive or negative correlation between A and B is 'spurious' if it disappears when other variables (C, D, etc.) are held constant. For example, a correlation between female sex and right-wing voting in a given population might disappear when age is held constant: that is, while a higher proportion of women than of men in the population vote for right-wing parties, there is no such difference between men and women of the same age. But the term 'spurious correlation' is misleading: 'spurious' correlations are real. The only reason for distinguishing 'spurious' and 'non-spurious' correlations relates, not to a correlation's reality, but to what inferences about causation can reasonably be made from it. The relation of correlation and causation will not be considered now, but will be taken up in the next chapter, on explanation in social science.

CHAPTER 4

Explanation in Social Science

Two broad issues arise in relation to the nature of explanation in social science. We saw in the first chapter how, in physical science, explanation depends on universal laws; whether this is also so in the social sciences is a much controverted question, which will be taken up later in this chapter.[1] Before that, however, we must discuss another controversial matter, namely, whether social science explanation is (in a sense to be elucidated) *individualistic*. The controversy about individualism, in fact, embraces, not only explanation, but the whole multi-faceted question of the relation of the individual to the social. This we must now examine.

The individual and the social

The controversy, or set of controversies, about the relation of the individual and the social, is one in which it is remarkably difficult to bring the various issues into clear focus. In broad terms, what is in dispute is the nature of social groups (or collectivities) and social institutions. Very roughly speaking, there are two sets of views, which can be labelled respectively 'individualist' and 'collectivist'. But there is also a terminological difficulty. Controversy has tended to take the form of arguments for and against so-called 'methodological individualism', a term apparently coined by Hayek and given wide currency through the work of Popper.[2] Unfortunately these writers and other contributors to the debate have defined this term in different ways, some of which explicitly exclude certain of the positions that fall on the individualistic side of the general division of opinion.[3] As a result, to

---

[1] See below, pp. 95 ff.

[2] See F. A. Hayek, *op. cit.*, p. 38; K. R. Popper, *The Poverty of Historicism*, p. 136, and *The Open Society and its Enemies* (London, Routledge and Kegan Paul paperback, 1962), vol. 2, p. 91.

[3] Thus Popper upholds 'methodological individualism' but rejects 'psychologism' – cf. pp. 106 ff. below.

dub someone a supporter or opponent of 'methodological individualism' does not convey a great deal. It seems best, therefore, to avoid the term as much as possible, and to consider instead the specific topics that arise.

According to Steven Lukes, in an article which attempts to disentangle some of these topics,[4] one of the issues is an *ontological* one, to do with the *reality* of social entities such as groups and institutions. Ontological individualism, which Lukes attributes to Popper and Hayek, denies the reality of these 'social wholes': 'in the social world only individuals are real'. Actually it is, I think, dubious whether Hayek or Popper, or anyone else, holds this view.[5] In any case it seems a very odd one. It can hardly be believed that social entities are unreal in the sense in which most people believe fairies to be unreal, or in which atheists believe God to be unreal. If there is some other sense in which they might be held to be unreal, it is so unclear that discussion of the topic appears unprofitable.

More worthy of discussion, however, is the question whether social entities have any reality *over and above* that of the individuals involved in them. Durkheim, for one, insisted that they do. 'Society', he wrote, 'is not a mere sum of individuals. Rather, the system formed by their association represents a specific reality which has its own characteristics.' Thus, 'the collective being is a being in its own right'. This applies not only to 'society', but to all social facts: 'Collective ways of acting or thinking have a reality outside the individuals who, at every moment of time, conform to them. These ways of thinking and acting exist in their own right. The individual finds them completely formed, and he cannot evade or change them.'[6]

Durkheim's assertion of the separate, individual-transcending reality of social phenomena has been widely influential, and is accepted by many social scientists. Durkheim himself, however, goes further. While he would admit that social facts partly manifest themselves in individual behaviour, many social facts, he holds, become quite *dissociated* from individual facts – as when legal rules are formulated and (often) written down, or religious beliefs are codified as articles of faith.[7] These

---

[4] 'Methological Individualism Reconsidered' in D. Emmet and A. MacIntyre (eds), *Sociological Theory and Philosophical Analysis* (London, Macmillan, 1970), pp. 76–88, esp. pp. 79–80.

[5] Hayek holds that social wholes 'are never given to our observation'; terms designating such wholes are really theories about the relations of individual events, and the wholes *exist* 'if, and to the extent to which' the corresponding theories are correct (*op. cit.*, pp. 54–5). Popper's position is less clear, but appears to be that social wholes are abstract or theoretical objects, not observable, but comparable to the theoretical entities of physical science (*The Poverty of Historicism*, pp. 135–6).

[6] See E. Durkheim, *The Rules of Sociological Method*, pp. 103, 124, lvi.

[7] *Ibid.*, pp. 7–8.

formulae exist as social facts even if individual behaviour does not apply them perfectly. What is more, according to Durkheim, it is this separability of social facts from individual facts that makes it possible to study social facts scientifically: 'Social facts lend themselves to objective representation in proportion as their separation from the individual facts expressing them is more complete'. Why? Because only through this separation do social facts become sufficiently *stable* to be observed. Individual manifestations of social facts, Durkheim believes, are too evanescent to be captured by a scientific study.[8]

Durkheim's position is clearly untenable. Even he himself is uncomfortably aware that what he calls 'objectified' representations of social facts (written law codes, articles of faith, etc.) may come to diverge greatly from 'the actual state of social relations'. Where there is reason to believe this has happened, Durkheim admits, they cannot be treated as social facts.[9] However, it is not easy to see how one could discover whether this divorce exists in a particular case, other than by comparing the formulae in question with the actual behaviour of individuals. The sociological usefulness of the formulae depends on knowledge of individual behaviour. Indeed it is generally accepted even by those who agree with Durkheim that a social fact is an individual-transcending reality, that it is the behaviour of individuals that provides the most powerful *evidence* as to the existence and characteristics of social facts. Nothing about social facts is *observable* except their individual manifestations.

This, however, does not in itself entail that a social fact simply *is* a set of facts about individuals; it may be that individual facts provide evidence for social facts without *being* them, in the same sort of way as people's behaviour and speech provides the most direct evidence available for their intentions and desires without *being* their intentions or desires. Let us formulate our problem more precisely. Are *social groups* simply individuals in certain relations to each other, or not? Likewise, are *social institutions* simply actions and attitudes of individuals related in particular ways?

What reason could there be to claim that social groups are other than individuals in particular relations? Durkheim asserts that 'the group thinks, feels, and acts quite differently from the way in which its members would if they were isolated'.[10] This is no more than a truism. If the members of a group were isolated they would not be related to one another in the ways that their group membership involves, and would necessarily act and think in ways different from those that result from (one might say, *are*) their relations as group members. This does not show that groups are other than interrelated individuals. But

---

[8] See E. Durkheim, *The Rules of Sociological Method*, pp. 44–6.
[9] *Ibid.*, p. 45n.   [10] *Ibid.*, p. 104.

Durkheim's argument becomes more than a truism when he maintains that social facts are *coercive* of individuals: 'the individual finds them completely formed, he cannot evade or change them,' but must simply conform to them. This puts the point too strongly, but it is true that the specific character of groups greatly influences their members. It can be argued further that the influence of a group on an individual member is not just the influence of several individuals on a single individual, for the group cannot be identified with the set of individuals who belong to it at a particular time. A group can persist, can maintain its identity, can even maintain its characteristics essentially unchanged, despite total replacement of its individual members.[11] It thus looks as if the group must be considered an entity separable from its individual members, an entity which confronts and moulds them.

Social groups and law
Some support for this view of groups comes from *legal* theory and practice. In many legal systems certain associations (notably 'corporations') are treated as legal 'persons' having rights and duties, and in particular as owning property which is distinct from that of their members or agents (only the corporate property is liable if the corporation acts in breach of its legal duty). That the law can so treat these groups may seem to suggest that they must indeed be entities different from any combination of individuals. However, the nature of the legal personality of groups has given rise to much controversy among jurists, some of which is instructive from our present point of view. So too is a parallel juristic debate on the nature of one particular kind of group – the State – and its relation to individuals. Some jurists have taken a position on these matters analogous to that of Durkheim, most notably the great legal scholar Otto Gierke.[12] They too have been impressed by the fact that corporations and States can outlive all the individuals who at any moment are their members.

Nevertheless, it is possible to give an account of these entities without supposing that they involve anything other than individuals (sometimes several generations of individuals) in particular relations. According to the jurist Hans Kelsen,[13] a State is constituted by the efficacy of a particular *legal order* (that is, system of laws) in relation to the inhabitants of a particular territory, and its continuity over time simply

[11] This argument follows closely Popper's account of 'holism' in *The Poverty of Historicism*, pp. 17–18.
[12] Gierke's views are summarized by F. W. Maitland in his Introduction to the former's *Political Theories of the Middle Age* (Cambridge U.P., 1900), pp. xxv–xxvii, and by H. Kelsen in *General Theory of Law and State* (New York, Russell and Russell, 1961), pp. 185–6. See also Gierke's *Political Theories of the Middle Age*, pp. 29–30 and pp. 67–72.
[13] *General Theory of Law and State*, pp. 181–92 and 96–109, esp. p. 98.

corresponds to the continued efficacy of the system of legal rules. In his account of corporate personality Kelsen applies a similar analysis to groups in general. Individuals form a group when there is a system of norms (i.e. rules) governing their mutual behaviour in certain respects; that such a group is accorded legal personality means that the law recognizes and accepts its system of rules, in particular rules specifying which individuals are 'organs' of the group, capable of acting on its behalf, required to act in fulfilment of its obligations, etc. That such a group has its own property simply means that its rules regulate the property rights and liabilities of its members in a particular way, which is accepted by the law.

Social rules

Kelsen's idea of groups as constituted by systems of *rules* governing aspects of the behaviour of individuals towards one another, while it helps to explain how groups can be accorded legal personality, is equally applicable to all groups whether they have this status or not. What Kelsen calls group 'organs' are incumbents of a particular sort of group *role* – a role being a functional complex of duties and rights all of which are laid by the rules of the group on any individual incumbent of that role.

Our analysis thus far has reduced social groups to individuals and systems of rules. Social institutions, too, are complexes of rules governing aspects of the behaviour of individuals. Our problem thus reduces to this question: can we give a full account of social rules (or norms) in terms only of the actions and attitudes of individuals? The well-known analysis of another jurist, H. L. A. Hart, shows that we can.[14] Hart analyses what is implied by the existence of a rule in a social group into 'external' and 'internal' elements, both fully individualistic: the external aspect is that people by and large behave as the rule says they ought, while the internal aspect is that some people at least (often a majority of the group) *consciously* take the rule as a standard for their own behaviour and that of others, and thus regard deviations from the rule as faults properly occasioning criticism and pressure for conformity. This 'internal' aspect of rules has in fact been used by one writer, Maurice Mandelbaum, to argue that 'societal facts' are *not* reducible to individual facts.[15] Mandelbaum stresses that the behaviour of individuals in their roles, and of others towards them, depends on their *awareness* of these roles (that is, roughly, of the rules that define them) – the social behaviour of individuals, in other words, depends on their thinking in terms of these 'societal facts'. Hence, Mandelbaum

[14] In his *The Concept of Law* (London, Oxford U.P., 1961), pp. 54–6.
[15] See M. Mandelbaum, 'Societal Facts', *British Journal of Sociology*, vol. VI (1955), pp. 307–9.

argues, any attempt to reduce the latter to purely individual facts must fail. This conclusion seems mistaken. That an individual thinks in terms of social concepts is an *individual* fact, not a social fact[16] – even if the individual is a sociologist or philosopher who believes that social facts are irreducible. Of course, he need not believe this – as Quentin Gibson points out,[17] he may (if he has considered the matter at all) take the view that the existence of a social role implies no more than certain attitudes and behaviour of individuals, of the sort picked out in Hart's analysis of social rules.

Characteristics of social wholes

What of the *characteristics* of social wholes? Is there any reason to think that these in some way transcend the characteristics of individuals, even if the social wholes themselves simply consist of individuals in particular relations? What is certainly true is that characteristics can be predicated of social entities that cannot be predicated of individuals. A society can be stratified, a polity oligarchical or democratic, while an individual cannot be said to be (in the same sense) any of these things. But this is a rather trivial point. A more controversial question is the *relation* between such 'social' predicates, and descriptions that can be given of individuals. The issue is the relation between kinds of *concepts* and *statements*. It can be posed in various ways, such as: can social predicates like 'stratified' and 'oligarchical' be *defined* in terms of individual predicates? Can statements describing social wholes (such as 'British society is highly stratified') be *deduced* from statements describing individuals only? Can statements describing social wholes be completely *translated* into statements describing individuals only?[18]

These formulations are sufficiently similar to be considered together. And here again, the anti-individualist position is untenable. For it can scarcely be denied that any social description implies the truth of several (often many) individual descriptions. Mandelbaum, for example, insists that this must be so – for otherwise it would not be possible to test social statements by observation and there could be no social science.[19] But in that case, the anti-individualist position must assert that social descriptions mean *more* than can be reproduced by the meaning of the individual descriptions. This has the following very strange implication.

---

[16] Just as a description of an individual's value-judgement is not itself a value-judgement but a statement of fact. Cf. p. 133 below.

[17] *Op. cit.*, pp. 104–5n.

[18] Cf., respectively, M. Brodbeck, 'Methodological Individualisms: Definition and Reduction' in W. H. Dray (ed.), *Philosophical Analysis and History* (New York, Harper and Row, 1966), pp. 299–300; Q. Gibson, *op. cit.*, pp. 98–9; M. Mandelbaum, *op. cit.*, pp. 309–10.

[19] *Op. cit.*, p. 312.

The meaning of a statement such as 'British society is oligarchic' must be divisible into two parts, one of which can be translated into statements describing the behaviour and attitudes of individuals and is observationally testable, while the other is not so translatable or testable. Let us suppose that the entire testable portion of this statement is appropriately translated, tested by observation, and found to be true. Does it then follow that British society is oligarchic? On the anti-individualist position, no – for 'British society is oligarchic' means something more than its testable partial translation. It is, on this view, perfectly possible that although all the individual manifestations of oligarchy are present in a society, nevertheless that society is not oligarchic.

But this is not only absurd in itself; it implies that the use of any social predicate (such as 'oligarchic') can in principle *never* be warranted by observable facts. To avoid this conclusion, one *must* take social descriptions as equivalent to specifiable individual behaviours, attitudes, etc.; and this implies that, if social statements are not actually identical in meaning to individual statements, they must at least be *deducible* from them.

Individualism and explanation

Our discussion so far has revealed no reason to think that social wholes and their characteristics are anything other than the characteristics and relations of individuals. But what about the *explanation* of facts about social wholes? According to one common definition, 'methodological individualism' is the doctrine that *all* social facts are in principle explicable individualistically – that is, solely in terms of facts about individuals. All references to other social facts are, on this view, in principle eliminable from such explanations. And indeed this must be so, if our argument so far is correct. If references to social facts are, as we have argued, essentially summary references to the characteristics and relations of individuals, any reference to a social fact that occurs in an explanation could in principle be replaced by references to the corresponding individual facts.

An example will perhaps make this clearer. What is the explanation of the (social) fact that, since at least 1945, there has been a two-party system in British politics (by contrast with other European parliamentary systems, where more than two parties have usually been important at any time)? This explanandum is the existence of a particular *social institution*, and one which involves the existence of *social groups*. A full explanation would doubtless be complex, but according to a well-known theory associated with Maurice Duverger, part of the explanation is another British political institution – the electoral system whereby British M.P.s are elected in single-member constituencies by simple majority on a single ballot.[20] But how does this electoral system help to explain the two-party system ? Duverger's theory depends on assumptions about the motives of the individuals involved – specifically, that party politicians seek power through governmental office, and that voters seek to maximize their influence over the choice of elected office-holders. Under the 'simple-majority, single-ballot' electoral system, it is relatively easy for a single party to monopolize governmental offices at any one time, while not more than two parties have a reasonable chance to do so; hence other parties tend to be abandoned by both voters and politicians. Thus, the British two-party system is explained as the outcome of the actions of individuals in a particular institutional setting. But the latter (the British electoral system) is, we have argued, itself nothing but the interdependent actions and attitudes of individuals. Hence Duverger's explanation of the British two-party system can in principle be made fully individualistic.

Duverger's theory also implies a general correlational *law*: 'The simple-majority single-ballot system favours the two-party system'.[21] If this correlation does indeed hold, then Duverger's theory provides a fully individualistic explanation of it also. Any general sociological law which is derived from an ideal typical theory[22] (such as Duverger's) is at the same time individualistically explained. Nor is it easy to see how else one might explain a sociological law. But is it possible that some sociological laws cannot be explained at all – that the conjunction of one sort of social fact with another may just be an ultimate datum ? This seems pretty unlikely. Not only could it never be *proved* that no individualistic explanation of such a conjunction could be found; some suggested candidates for irreducibly social laws patently fail to fit the bill. For instance, Ernest Nagel[23] has pointed to Keynesian macroeconomics, which asserts relations between large-scale economic aggregates that are *not* derived from the 'neo-classical' micro-economic analysis in terms of individual preferences. An example is the second law in the list in chapter 3; it asserts relations between 'government expenditure', 'taxation', 'aggregate demand', and 'unemployment'.[24] But not only are these aggregates in principle easily decomposable into actions of, and facts about, individuals; the law is, like all the Keynesian laws, explicitly derived from postulates about individuals – about their 'marginal propensity to consume', their preference for 'liquidity', and their expectations as to future yields from capital assets.[25]

---

[20] See his *Political Parties* (London, Methuen, 1954), pp. 208, 216–28.
[21] *Ibid.*, p. 217.   [22] Cf. above, pp. 58 ff.
[23] *Op. cit.*, pp. 543–4.   [24] See above, p. 53.
[25] J. M. Keynes, *The General Theory of Employment, Interest and Money* (London, Macmillan, 1936), pp. 246–7. Cf. the similar argument in J. W. N.

Even if it is accepted that social facts and social laws are in principle explicable individualistically, there remains a further controversial question about the relation of the individual and the social – namely, the *relative explanatory ultimacy* of psychological (that is, individual) and social facts. For it may be that facts of individual psychology (people's propensities to behave in particular ways) are in turn dependent on social facts. Hence it may be denied that the *ultimate* explanations of social facts are facts of individual psychology, or in other words, that social science is *reducible* to psychology. It will, however, be convenient to postpone consideration of this question[26] till we have discussed the relation between social facts and laws.

The explanation of action

We saw at the beginning of this chapter that one of the controversial questions about explanation of social facts is whether, like explanation in physical science, it depends on laws. Social facts, however, are simply the inter-related actions and attitudes of individuals. What, then, is the logic of explanation of human action?

The proffering of explanations for people's behaviour goes on incessantly in everyday life. Let us try to analyse the structure of these explanations through an imaginary example. Suppose that a man of hitherto blameless character has embezzled money. Why did he do so? At his trial, it emerges that he was heavily in debt and short of funds. This situation, it would appear, explains his embezzlement – was, we might say, the *reason* for his action.

What does this imply? First, that the man was *aware* of the situation – a situation of which a person is unaware cannot provide him with a reason for acting. Indeed, from the point of view of how a person will act, it makes no difference whether any given situation actually exists, so long as he *believes* it to exist. In the present imaginary case, we ought strictly to say that the man embezzled because he believed himself to be in debt and short of money. It is only because we assume that people are normally aware of such facts that we can say, elliptically, that he embezzled because of his objective situation.

Is the logical structure of this explanation like that of physical phenomena – either of the commonsense or of the scientific variety? It certainly does not seem to be like that of physical science explanation. If it were, it would imply at least the first and possibly both of the following universal laws: 'Whenever a man (believes he) is unable to

Watkins, 'Methodological Individualism: A Reply', in rebuttal of M. Brodbeck, 'On the Philosophy of the Social Sciences', both in J. O'Neill (ed.), *Modes of Individualism and Collectivism* (London, Heinemann, 1973), pp. 182 and 109 respectively.

[26] Discussed below, pp. 106–8.

pay his debts, he steals money'; and 'Whenever a man steals money, he (believes he) is unable to pay his debts'. Both of these laws are obviously false; yet their falsity in no way weakens the explanation. Nevertheless, there is a widespread view that such explanations at least approximate closely in structure to physical science explanations; that they depend, if not on universal laws, at least on probabilistic ones, to the effect that in a situation of the sort cited in explanation, people *usually* perform an action of the sort in question. Yet the laws suggested above are almost certainly not even probabilistically true; and this, if it is so, still does not weaken the explanation.

Why, then, the widespread view that explanations of actions depend on generalizations? One reason, perhaps, is that it *is* often possible to generalize about how people behave in given circumstances; hence, it may appear that an action that *conforms* to such a generalization *depends* on that generalization for its explanation. A. J. Ayer, for example, suggests that, if we explain that a man put on an overcoat to go out because it was winter, 'our explanation derives its force from some such presupposition as that people in general under conditions of this kind do what they can to protect themselves against the cold'.[27] Again, Patrick Gardiner claims that 'we can explain a man's action on being threatened by a blackmailer . . . in terms of a generalization about how people react when their interests are threatened'.[28] Now, it may be that when people go out of doors in cold weather they generally put on warm clothing; but what do they generally do when threatened by a blackmailer? Some comply with his demands; some go to the police. *It is not necessary to know which is the typical reaction in order to explain a man's action as due to blackmail.* A man may give another money because the latter blackmailed him; a man may go to the police because another blackmailed him; a man may even kill another because the latter blackmailed him. Each action can equally be explained by a blackmailer's threat, whether the action is a typical response or a very unusual one. As Hart and Honoré put it, in a passage worth quoting at length, if a person asserts that he acted in a particular way because of threats,

'. . . it would be absurd to call upon him to show that there really was this connexion between the threats and his action, by showing that generally he or other persons complied when threats were made . . . The question, whether or not a given person acted on a

[27] A. J. Ayer, 'Man as a Subject for Science' in P. Laslett and W. G. Runciman (eds), *Philosophy, Politics and Society, Third Series* (Oxford, Blackwell, 1967), pp. 16–17.
[28] P. Gardiner, *The Nature of Historical Explanation* (London, Oxford U.P. paperback, 1968), p. 50.

given occasion for a given reason, is primarily a question as to the way in which the agent reached his decision to do the act in question: whether the thought of a given reason weighed with him as he made up his mind, and whether or not in doing the action he consciously adapted the manner of its execution accordingly.'[29]

This, I believe, is essentially correct, but it does suggest a difficulty. How can one know what went on in a man's mind? Action explanations, on the Hart and Honoré view, imply statements about unobservable mental processes. The hostility of empiricists to such statements is doubtless another reason for the doctrine that explanations of actions in terms of the agent's situation rest, not on assumptions about his mental processes, but on a generalization about how people usually behave in that situation. And yet, whatever the difficulties of justifying or testing a statement about mental processes, it remains true that this is what is involved in the explanation of action. How men generally behave in given types of situation may suggest a hypothesis for the explanation of an action, but cannot be conclusive as to its truth or falsity. It is perfectly possible that a man in a given situation acts as people usually do in that situation, and yet not because of it. It is even logically possible (however unlikely) that people in a given situation *always* act in a given way, but *never* because of that situation.

Explanation-sketches
Let us look now at one of the best-known and most detailed arguments in favour of the view that action-explanations rest on implicit generalizations. Carl Hempel, in an article on explanation in history,[30] discusses the question: why did many farmers migrate from Oklahoma to California in the early decades of this century? They did so because, as Hempel says, continual drought and sandstorms had made their existence increasingly precarious, and California seemed to them to offer better living conditions. According to Hempel, this explanation implies some general regularity of human behaviour, but, as is often the case, it is not easy to state it in a form that accords with the known facts. The implied regularity is perhaps, Hempel says, something like 'Populations tend to migrate to regions which offer better living conditions'; but unfortunately this is so vague that it is impossible to say whether the evidence supports it. A more specific version would be:

29 H. L. A. Hart and A. M. Honoré, 'Causal Judgment in History and in the Law', in W. H. Dray (ed.), *Philosophical Analysis and History*, p. 234. The passage is reprinted from Hart and Honoré, *Causation in the Law* (Oxford U.P., 1959).
30 'The Function of General Laws in History', in P. Gardiner (ed.), *Theories of History* (Glencoe, Free Press, 1959), pp. 349–51.

embezzlement does not imply that the man habitually embezzles or steals whenever he has debts he cannot pay. For one thing, he may be in this situation only once in his life – in which case the explanandum cannot be deduced from any statement of his habitual behaviour. But this is not decisive; what is decisive is that the explanation does *not* imply that if the same circumstances occurred on another occasion the man would act similarly. To quote Hart and Honoré again: 'The question, whether or not a given person acted on a given occasion for a given reason is primarily a question as to how the agent reached his decision to do the act in question' – not how he would act on other similar occasions, if any.

Explanation by motive
So far, we have discussed explanation of actions in terms of what was earlier called the agent's *reason* for acting – that is, the occasioning circumstances of the action – and have found no reason to think that action-explanations rest on or imply anything similar to the universal laws of physical science. But it is too soon to conclude that physical explanations and action-explanations are radically different. For something else is involved in explaining actions besides reasons in this sense. When, in our earlier example, it was said that a man embezzled money because he was unable to pay his debts, this explanation did not specify (because of its obviousness) his *motive* for the embezzlement – which, clearly, was that he wanted to escape from his indebted situation. But this is of course part of the explanation of his action – had he not wanted to escape from his indebtedness (and, one must again add, *believed* that by embezzling he could escape it) he would not have embezzled.

When we take into account the motive component of action-explanation, does it turn out to be, after all, similar to the explanation of physical phenomena? This has frequently been argued.[35] Thus, it may be said, if one explains an act of embezzlement by the agent's desire to escape from debt, one presupposes something like the following law:

'When a person believes an action to be a means of bringing about a state of affairs he desires, he performs that action.'

From this law, together with the further premises that the man wished to escape from his indebtedness and believed he could do so by embezzling, it can be deduced that he would embezzle. Unfortunately,

35 See, for example, Q. Gibson, *op. cit.*, pp. 30–2; A. J. Ayer, *op. cit.*, pp. 19–21; A. Pap, *Introduction to the Philosophy of Science* (Glencoe, Free Press, 1962), pp. 263–7.

'Most people who live in a region that seems to them to offer living conditions inferior to those offered by some other region migrate to the latter'. But this law is very likely false. If so, Hempel would argue, the explanation given above of the migration of the Oklahoma farmers is not, after all, a full-fledged explanation, but only an *explanation-sketch*; that is, a rough indication of the situation which caused the migration. A full-fledged explanation would require that the relevant situation be specified in sufficient detail to show the case in question to be an instance of a universal or nearly universal law. Thus, the situation relevant to explaining the migration from Oklahoma is not fully described in terms of the mere contrast apparent to the migrants between living conditions in Oklahoma and in California; a complete specification would perhaps include the further points that the contrast appeared to them a very marked one, that California was easily accessible and sparsely populated, that no way was apparent of improving living conditions in Oklahoma, etc.

Hempel's conception of an explanation-sketch seems rather similar to what in chapter one was called the *common-sense* type of physical explanation.[31] A common-sense causal assertion, we saw, implies a *vague* law, to the effect that in certain circumstances, presumed to have been present on the occasion in question but not necessarily specifiable in practice, an event similar to the 'cause' is always followed by an event similar to the 'effect'. Similarly Hempel's argument holds that explanation of an action implies that circumstances existed, even if they cannot actually be specified, in which such an action always (or nearly always) occurs.

But explanations of actions do not, in fact, imply even such vague laws. Whether or not human beings have free will, we do not expect them all to react to similar circumstances in the same way – not even to similar circumstances of which they are aware.[32] Some reactions to given circumstances are unusual, but are no less explicable in terms of these circumstances than more usual reactions. The Oklahomans' migration may have been a common enough reaction to their situation, specified in adequate detail; but an action such as, say, murder, is probably not a usual reaction to any situation, but can still be explained as a reaction to a situation – as the earlier discussion of possible responses to blackmail indicates.

Individualistic laws

The discussion so far suggests, perhaps, that the major defect of the regularity interpretation of action-explanations is its failure to do

[31] See above, pp. 25–6.
[32] This is because of differences in *motives* (i.e., goals, and beliefs as to how to achieve them). Cf. below, pp. 88 ff.

justice to the inte... [rnal]
it might be argued that a m...
for individuality, and so assimilate a...
explanations of physical phenomena. For ph...
some extent be treated as individuals, in somewhat...
human beings – that is, can be described and understood in...
their own peculiar characteristics, rather than those they share with other similar objects. For example, the owner of, say, a radio-set soon enough gets to know its particular 'personality'. Perhaps the sound sometimes fades, but can regularly be restored by tapping it in a certain way (such idiosyncracies of machines are far from rare). Even if the owner knows nothing about radio electronics, he can still in a sense explain to one unfamiliar with the radio why, in a particular case, its sound returned; it did so, he might explain, because the radio was tapped in the appropriate way. And he may have in mind, as justification for his explanation, not any law about machines in general, but only a 'law' about the particular radio: 'When this radio is tapped in a particular way, its sound is (always or usually) restored'. For this individualistic law can serve as the major premise of an explanatory deduction:

Major premise: When this radio is tapped, its sound is restored.

Minor premise: This radio was tapped.

Conclusion: This radio's sound was restored.

This explanation is logically just as satisfactory as one that depends on a universal general law; both proceed by deduction from a regularity that subsumes the explanandum.[33] The highly general universal laws that physical science seeks permit one sort of subsuming explanation of particular facts ('scientific explanation'); but other sorts are possible. Does explanation of human actions depend on individualistic laws – and thus, after all, on regularities? According to Patrick Gardiner, it is to show how it fits into the pattern of the agent's normal behaviour, of how he normally behaves under given circumstances.[34] But this is not so. Of course, an individual's behaviour will to some extent fall into such patterns – otherwise the concepts of 'character' and 'personality' would be meaningless; and much individual behaviour will conform to these patterns. But such patterns are not necessary for explaining particular actions. Take our earlier example of the embezzler: the explanation given for the

[33] Cf. Gilbert Ryle's account of dispositional explanations in *The Concept of Mind* (London, Penguin, 1963), pp. 43, 86–8.
[34] *The Nature of Historical Explanation*, pp. 124–5.

however, the suggested law is far from satisfactory. Firstly, as it stands it is untrue. A person may be aware of several alternative ways of realizing a desired state of affairs – obviously he will not then perform all of them. We might therefore amend the law, as follows:

'When a person believes an action to be the best means available of bringing about a state of affairs he desires, he performs that action'.

But now the law is ambiguous. Does the 'best means' mean the easiest or most efficient means? If so, the law is still untrue. Often, a person will not choose the most efficient means, from moral motives. He may even from moral motives eschew all possible means, or the only possible means, to a desired end. Most people, for example, who found themselves in the position of our imaginary embezzler and like him wished to escape from indebtedness, would not resort to criminal action even if no other way of escape seemed open. A person may, in other words, have *conflicting* motives in relation to a possible action. He may have imcompatible desires, between which he must *choose* – for example, the desire to escape from indebtedness, and the desire not to act criminally. The embezzler in our example might perfectly well have had such conflicting motives.

Decision-schemes
The situation we have been discussing can be summed up as follows. At any time, an agent has a particular set of attitudes (pro and con) to various existing and possible states of affairs, and a particular set of beliefs about his situation and the possible, probable or certain consequences of various actions that he might perform. This set of attitudes and beliefs has been called by J. W. N. Watkins a *decision-scheme*.[36] Our question now is: what is the relation between a person's decision-scheme and his action? Certainly it is by reference to elements of the agent's decision-scheme of the moment that we normally explain an action. Does this mean that his decision-scheme *determines* his action? That whenever a person has a particular decision-scheme he performs a particular action? And is this last the general form of the *laws* on which all action-explanations rest?

The answer given even by such upholders of the regularity interpretation of action-explanation as Watkins, Popper, and Hempel is 'not quite'. According to these writers, an agent's decision-scheme dictates what he will do if he acts rationally.[37] A decision-scheme does imply

[36] See his 'Imperfect Rationality' in R. Borger and F. Cioffi (eds), *Explanation in the Behavioural Sciences* (Cambridge U.P., 1970), pp. 206–8.
[37] Cf. J. W. N. Watkins, 'Imperfect Rationality' in R. Borger and F. Cioffi (eds), *Explanation in the Behavioural Sciences*, pp. 172–6, 206–10; K. R. Popper,

what the agent, in the light of his aims and beliefs, should do; but he will not do this unless he draws the appropriate conclusion from his scheme. And he may fail to do so, if the scheme is complex, or if he acts hastily or under the pressure of emotion, of if he simply lacks sufficient intelligence.[38] Thus, on this view, the explanation of an action in terms of the relevant elements of a decision-scheme assumes the agent was rational at the time (i.e. was capable of inferring the appropriate 'practical conclusion' from his decision-scheme). And such explanations do, it is claimed, rest on laws. For Hempel, the general form of such explanations is as follows:

Premise 1: The agent was in a particular situation and had a particular decision-scheme.

Premise 2: The agent was rational at the time.

Premise 3: In such a situation any rational agent who has such a decision-scheme will do x.

Conclusion: The agent did x.

According to Hempel (and also Popper and Watkins), the third premise in this deductive scheme is a descriptive generalization, and any explanation of the sort we are discussing implies that a generalization of this form is true. This, we might say, is Hempel's second attempt to state the law implied by action-explanations, by virtue of which they can be exhibited as similar in logical structure to physical science explanations.

But this attempt, too, fails. For, firstly, it is not normally the case that an agent's decision-scheme unequivocally dictates a unique rational conclusion as to how to act, *even if the scheme itself is quite firm and coherent*. This is due to the heterogeneity of the elements of decision-schemes, which (as we have seen) are likely to include *inter alia* both moral principles and self-regarding desires. The decision-scheme of someone in the situation of our embezzler may include both the desire to escape from indebtedness, and a morally based reluctance to steal. In the end either self-interest or moral principle might prevail, and it does not seem reasonable to say that one decision would be

---

The Open Society and its Enemies, vol. 2, pp. 97 and 265; C. G. Hempel, 'Rational Action', *Proceedings and Addresses of the American Philosophical Association*, vol. XXV (1962), pp. 10–23, and 'Explanation in Science and in History' in W. H. Dray (ed.), *Philosophical Analysis and History*, pp. 115–24.

[38] Cf. C. G. Hempel, 'Rational Action', *Proceedings and Addresses of the American Philosophical Association*, vol. XXV (1962), pp. 17–18.

rational, the other not. *Either* decision, however, would be explicable in terms of (different) elements of the agent's decision-scheme. As Hart and Honoré point out, action-explanations imply that, in the agent's decision to act, certain elements of his decision-scheme weighed with him and guided his decision, not that he acted rationally.

Secondly, even if we were to waive this point, and accept that an agent's decision-scheme dictates a unique rational action (and this will sometimes be the case, where there is no conflict between the sense of obligation and the pursuit of self-interest), Hempel's third premise, instead of being false, would now be equivalent to a tautology. For a 'rational agent' is one who decides to act, and therefore acts, as his decision-scheme dictates. (If this is not so, Hempel's third premise becomes false again.) Even if an agent does not act with full rationality, in Hempel's sense, it is frequently quite possible to explain his action in terms of *some* elements of his decision-scheme.

There is still no reason to believe that an action-explanation implies the deducibility of the explanandum from a set of premises that includes anything like a law of nature. Correspondingly, nothing is involved in these explanations which is a *cause* of the explanandum in the Humean sense (analysed in the first chapter). A motive explains an action, not through subsumption under a regular conjunction, much less through showing it to be inevitable, but through rendering it *intelligible*. The relation between physical causes and their effects is not intelligible – in principle, any sort of event could (logically speaking) be the cause of any other, it is only a matter of brute fact what the actual causal relations of the world are. By contrast, a desire can *in principle* explain *only* an action believed by the agent to be conducive to its realization, for by its very meaning that is the only kind of action that it can render intelligible.

Intentions

Let us briefly consider now one final attempt to salvage the regularity interpretation of action-explanations. Reverting to our embezzlement example, it could be argued that what really explains that action is not that the embezzler *wanted* to be free from debt (as we saw, he might have wanted this, but not embezzled), but that he *intended* to bring about his freedom from debt (and believed embezzlement was the best or only means to do so). The following deductive argument might be constructed:

Premise 1: Whenever a person believes an action to be the best or only means to bring about a situation he intends to bring about, and is able to perform that action, he performs it.

Premise 2: The agent intended to free himself from debt.

Premise 3: The agent believed embezzlement to be the best or only means to free himself from debt.

Premise 4: The agent was able to embezzle.

Conclusion: The agent embezzled.

Here, of course, Premise 1 is supposedly the regularity statement. But in fact it is tautological, as is shown by the fact that the explanandum can be deduced from Premises 2, 3, and 4, without help from the first premise.[39] Or at least, if Premises 2, 3, and 4 do not together actually entail the conclusion, their connection with the conclusion is, as von Wright says, *logical* rather than causal, in the sense that the criterion for *verifying* that an agent believes a given action to be the best available means of realizing a state of affairs he intends to bring about is that, given the opportunity, he performs that action.[40]

The justification of action-explanations
According to our account, the explanation of an action is a matter of the agent's beliefs and motives at the time, that is, of factors unobservable by anyone else. How, then, can one justify a particular explanation of another's action – how defend it against a challenge, or choose between rival explanations? Among scholars it is above all historians who have to face this problem. We have argued that how the agent or others behave on other similar occasions is not a decisive test, so the study of similar instances, which serves as a check on physical explanations, apparently cannot be used in relation to actions. In some cases (by no means all) the agent's own testimony may be available, but it is not necessarily to be trusted. Indeed, if Freudian theory is to be believed, an agent may even himself be deceived as to his true motive for his action; the true motive may operate at an *unconscious* level. Again, according to the Marxist doctrine of false consciousness, people who (for example) conceive themselves to be pursuing ideal values (such as 'liberty') may in reality be defending their class interests. There is no space here to assess the validity of these theoretical conceptions, but in view of the commonsense concept of self-deception and the other points adduced above, it is clear that we cannot simply rely on agents' own explanations of their actions.

[39] Cf. the argument of Alan Donagan in 'Alternative Historical Explanations and their Verification', *The Monist*, vol. 53 (1969), pp. 58–98.

[40] G. H. von Wright, *Explanation and Understanding* (London, Routledge and Kegan Paul, 1971), pp. 93, 107, 115.

The explanation of another person's action is like physical science explanation to this extent, that it must be in the last resort hypothetical. An explanatory hypothesis may be drawn from various sources – the agent's own explanation (if any), or knowledge of his character, or of his particular culture or sub-culture, or of human motives in general. If possible the hypothesis must be *tested* by examining other actions of the agent at about the same period of his life, to see if they too appear to reflect the hypothesized motive. The hypothesis to be preferred, in other words, is that which best fits this evidence. But it must be recognized that, if our argument so far is sound, it is possible that a hypothetical explanation is correct, although *no* other action of the agent is similarly motivated. We have to assume that, though this is possible, it is unlikely – in other words that there is usually a degree of stability in the purposes people pursue, and that these purposes guide a series of actions over a period of time.[41] It is on the grounds that it is 'belied by his actions' in this sense that we may feel justified in rejecting the agent's own account of his motives in favour of another hypothesis; and even in concluding that he is deceived or is deceiving himself as to his motives. An instructive case in point is reported in a study of the Norwegian judiciary.[42] It seems that the sentences imposed by some judges vary with the social class of the offender, although the judges assert and perhaps sincerely believe that they seek to apply the law impartially. Yet the facts (if correctly reported) show beyond reasonable doubt that in the sentences of such a judge unacknowledged motives are at work.

Action, psychology, and physical science

Because of the uncertainties attaching to explanation in terms of 'motives' and 'reasons', it is not surprising that some writers advocate abandoning this whole language and replacing it by one more amenable to handling in the manner of physical science. Prominent among them is the psychologist B. F. Skinner.[43] For Skinner, it is a mistake to say that a man acted *because of* some desire or purpose, or *in order to* bring about some desired result. Rather, explanations of actions should be in terms of 'contingencies of reinforcement'. Skinner holds that certain types of actions have consequences which in certain circumstances are positively or negatively reinforcing, that is, make it more or less likely that in similar circumstances in future a person will perform a similar

[41] Cf. A. Donagan, 'The Popper-Hempel Thesis Reconsidered', in W. H. Dray (ed.), *Philosophical Analysis and History*, pp. 151–3.
[42] See T. Burns, 'Sociological Explanation', in D. Emmet and A. MacIntyre (eds), *Sociological Theory and Philosophical Analysis*, pp. 64–5.
[43] See, for example, B. F. Skinner, *Beyond Freedom and Dignity* (London, Cape, 1972), pp. 8–10, 27–8, 45, 72, 94–6, 108–9, 170.

action. Also, different states of affairs can through a person's individual experience become associated, and in this way a consequence not at first reinforcing can become so, through association with a reinforcing consequence. Since different individuals have different experiences, they will thus, to some extent, find different things reinforcing. It is in these terms that actions are to be explained. To say that someone acted in order to bring about a certain result is to indicate, in misleading and unscientific language, that in the past his performing such an action has been followed by the result in question, and the result in question is positively reinforcing to him – that is, increases the likelihood of his performing the action that brings it about.

But it is easy to see that this analysis is mistaken. When we say that a man embezzled in order to escape from debt, we certainly do not indicate thereby that this is a sort of behaviour which has been reinforced in him through past experiences of its consequences. On the contrary he may never have performed such an action before. If he did, its consequences may have been disastrous (to repeat a mistake is neither impossible nor inexplicable). There is no need to deny that the probabilities of people performing various actions is much affected by the 'contingencies of reinforcement' they have experienced, nor that the manipulation of these contingencies offers, as Skinner believes, the most promising basis for rational social control. It may be, too, that the Skinnerian contingencies are required *in order to explain agents' motives and intentions*. What must be insisted on, however, is that explanations of actions in terms of motive and intention make no reference to these contingencies, are perfectly valid in their own right, and can be given when the contingencies are (as they usually are) unknown.

That explanation of actions by reasons and motives is valid in its own right does not imply, either, that human beings are somehow not subject to physical laws – even if, despite present appearances to the contrary, matter conforms to deterministic universal laws. Every action involves some bodily movements, subject, we may assume, to the laws of physiology and ultimately of physics, and in principle explicable in terms of these laws. But as we saw in chapter 2, a given *sort* of action does not correspond to a particular sort (or series) of bodily movements – voting, for example, may be performed by marking a cross on paper, by raising one's arm, etc.[44] The explanation of why a man voted for or against some proposal or candidate, in terms of reasons and motives, would not normally depend on which particular bodily movements were involved in the action; but the physical explanation of an arm rising must obviously be greatly different from that of a hand moving a pencil in such a way as to mark a cross. It is, in other words, possible

[44] See above, p. 45.

to look at human beings from two different points of view – as matter, and as agents. Each has its appropriate method of explanation. To seek the reasons and motives for action expresses, not an interest in scientific uniformities, but, as William Dray has put it, 'a humane curiosity, an interest in discovering and reconstructing the lives of [other] people'.[45]

Explanation and laws in social science

In this chapter we have so far argued, first, that social facts are simply the related actions and attitudes of individuals, and second, that the explanation of actions is radically different from physical explanation in that it implies no regularities or laws. This strongly suggests that the explanation of social facts must also differ in a similar way from physical explanation. Nevertheless, as we have already noted, many philosophers and social scientists believe strongly in the fundamental similarity of all the sciences, so it is not surprising that there is a considerable party that denies any such difference in the *scientific* explanation of physical and social facts. Their argument is, briefly, that physical science provides a model for explanation that can be applied in social science, thus by-passing all need to refer to reasons and motives for actions – concepts to which they are in any case hostile on empiricist grounds.

Is there any justification for this view? Empiricists emphasize that the successful development of an explanatory science requires the evolution of unfamiliar concepts in place of 'pre-scientific' ways of explaining. In fact, some claim, it was only by abandoning concepts appropriate to the explanation of action that genuine scientific explanation of *physical* phenomena could develop at all.[46] Some of these pre-scientific explanatory concepts were religious: physical events might be attributed to the desires of gods or spirits (for example, a natural disaster such as an earthquake might be explained by God's wish to punish sinners). Some were philosophical and in particular Aristotelian: Skinner cites the idea that a falling body accelerates because it becomes increasingly 'jubilant' as it approaches the earth, considered by Aristotelians to be its natural position. Some, again, belonged to pre-scientific common sense: according to Lundberg, it was once normal to suppose that the fall of a tree over a path might be a malicious act on the tree's part, performed in order to block one's progress. These are all explanations of physical phenomena in terms of a mind, attributed either to physical objects themselves, or to an invisible power that

[45] 'The Historical Explanation of Action Reconsidered' in S. Hook (ed.) *Philosophy and History* (New York U.P., 1963), pp. 132–3.
[46] Cf. B. F. Skinner, *op. cit.*, pp. 5–10; G. A. Lundberg, *op. cit.*, pp. 39–46, 56–7.

controls them. Empiricists draw the moral that the social sciences, like the physical sciences, can and should cease to use mental concepts in explanation, replacing them by genuinely scientific explanations based on laws.

This argument is not convincing. That explanation in terms of reasons and motives is inappropriate to physical phenomena by no means shows that it is not appropriate in the social sphere. Very probably, explanation of human action being the most familiar and obvious and perhaps the earliest sort of explanation of which men had experience, that pattern of explanation was extended by analogy to physical phenomena when *their* explanation came in question. This analogical extrapolation has been unfruitful, because it postulates the existence of minds for which there is no evidence. By contrast, all our experience of social intercourse assures us that human beings do have minds – do, in other words, act for reasons and from motives.

Nevertheless, in view of the difficulties already noted in establishing action-explanations, it is worthwhile to investigate whether it is possible to explain social facts according to what we may call the 'positivist' programme, that is, in terms of regularities instead of reasons and motives. We can once again take Durkheim as representative of this programme: his view is that explanation of social facts must be 'deterministic', not 'purposive'.[47] To explain a social fact is, for Durkheim, to find its *cause*; and 'the determining cause of a social fact should be sought among the social facts preceding it and not among the states of the individual consciousness' such as motives or intentions – 'questions of intention are too subjective to allow of scientific treatment'.[48] How does one establish that a relation of cause and effect holds between two social facts? As with any two facts, one does so by 'comparing the cases in which they are . . . present or absent, to see if the variations they present in these different combinations of circumstances indicate that one depends on the other'.[49] In other words, attribution of cause depends on regularities. Where social facts are concerned, the regularities that can be discovered are, in Durkheim's view, of the kind that John Stuart Mill called 'concomitant variations'.[50] Now, according to Mill, two phenomena vary concomitantly if one of them 'varies in any manner' whenever the other 'varies in some particular manner', in which case the two are causally connected.[51] Mill seems here to be referring to universal laws of functional dependence, such as Newton's Law of Gravitation (according to which the gravitational attraction between two bodies varies as the product of their masses). Durkheim, however, takes Mill's concomitant variations to be *correla-*

[47] E. Durkheim, *The Rules of Sociological Method*, p. 93.
[48] *Ibid.*, pp. 110 and 95.   [49] *Ibid.*, p. 125.   [50] *Ibid.*, pp. 129–34.
[51] See his *System of Logic* (London, 1862), vol. I, Bk. III, ch. VIII, §6.

tions (although, as we saw,[52] only *perfect* correlations *of cardinal data* are equivalent to such laws). In essence, Durkheim's view is that a social fact can be explained only by pointing out another, antecedently existing social fact, such that the two sorts of social fact are positively correlated.

Let us now see how Durkheim's explanatory method works in practice. He himself gives an example of two positively correlated social facts, namely suicide rate and educational level.[53] That is: a community with a higher average level of education than another more often has a higher than a lower rate of suicide; and vice-versa. (This is a rank-order or ordinal correlation.)[54] There is, of course, no way to show that this holds (or 'probably' holds) as an unrestrictedly general correlational law; but even supposing that it does, can one infer a causal link between education and suicide? Not yet, as Durkheim himself recognizes. There remains the problem of so-called 'spurious' correlation: that is, correlation between variables due, not to a causal relation between them, but to one between each of them and some third variable. According to Durkheim, a third variable is in fact responsible for the correlation of suicide and education, namely 'the weakening of religious traditionalism',[55] or (more briefly) secularization. There are, in other words, three positive correlations: between suicide and secularization, between education and secularization, and between education and suicide. But, Durkheim maintains, there is no causal connection between education and suicide: it is secularization that leads to both these phenomena. That is, he asserts that in any community which is secularized to any appreciable degree, and in which there is both suicide and educational activity, at least *part* of its suicide rate and of its total educational activity is explained by its secularization. Durkheim does not mean to imply that if it were not secularized at all, it would necessarily have no suicide and no education at all; but if it were less secularized, it would, 'other things remaining equal', have less suicide and less education as a result.

Why is Durkheim so sure that secularization causes suicide, while education does not? His own justification is the following: it is not possible to understand how education could lead to suicide, while it *is* possible to understand how secularization can do so. Why? Because (Durkheim explicitly says) there is no possible psychological process whereby the acquisition of knowledge could weaken the instinctive desire for self-preservation; whereas (presumably) there *is* an imaginable psychological process whereby the loss of a traditional religion

---

[52] Above, p. 71. [53] *The Rules of Sociological Method*, pp. 131–2.
[54] See above, p. 68.
[55] It is to be noted that this account in *The Rules of Sociological Method* differs considerably from that given by Durkheim in *Suicide*.

could do so. Without examining too critically the plausibility of Durkheim's arguments here, the important point to note is that, despite his overt hostility to taking account of the mental life of individuals, he finds it necessary, in order to interpret the explanatory significance of correlations, to do precisely that.

Is it in fact necessary? As a matter of fact statistical techniques developed since Durkheim wrote would make it possible to test which of his three correlations correspond to causal connections. Broadly, this involves the holding constant of one variable to see if the correlation between the other two remains. If Durkheim is right, in communities secularized to an equal degree there is no positive correlation between education and suicide; but in communities with equal suicide rates there is a positive correlation between secularization and education; and in communities with the same average level of education there is a positive correlation between suicide and secularization.

But it must be stressed that while, assuming that all relevant correlations are known, statistical tests can indicate between which pairs of factors causal relations hold, they cannot establish the *direction* of causation.[56] Supposing the results of such tests to be compatible with Durkheim's thesis, it then may be the case that (1) secularization causes both suicide and education, or (2) education and suicide both cause secularization, or (3) education causes secularization and secularization causes suicide, or (4) suicide causes secularization and secularization causes education (in addition to reciprocal causation). In order to establish which is actually the case, it would be natural to use the method Durkheim found himself forced to employ; that is, to see whether it is possible to reconstruct a plausible causal chain connecting two factors in terms of influences on people's motives and reasons for action. In these terms, incidentally, the third possibility above seems as plausible as the first, which is Durkheim's assertion. On the other hand, suicide can be ruled out as a cause of either of its correlates.

Up to a point, the situation in physical science is similar to that in social science. As we saw in the first chapter, not even a perfect correlation of A and B proves that A causes B, rather than vice-versa. But physical science can usually infer the direction of causation from the order of succession: cause precedes effect. In social science the same principle holds, but is extremely hard to apply. Secularization, for example, is not an event, but a lengthy process. It is not possible to pinpoint the time at which a given amount of secularization occurred, and to observe whether a certain number of suicides took place after some appropriate time-lag (which anyway could not be calculated).

Not only is it difficult or even impossible in the social sciences to

[56] Cf. H. M. Blalock, Jr., *An Introduction to Social Research* (Englewood Cliffs, Prentice-Hall, 1970), pp. 68–72.

gauge the explanatory significance of correlations alone; not only can their explanatory significance sometimes be elucidated by taking account of people's motives and reasons for acting; but a correlation which is not intelligible in these terms cannot explain a social fact. Secularization is not itself a motive nor a reason for suicide; but it explains suicide only in so far as it gives people motives and reasons for suicide. Durkheim's main idea is probably that secularization deprives the individual of certain aids and resources which help to make personal disasters bearable; it thus weakens people's motives for continuing to live, and makes these disasters, in some cases, a reason for suicide. Similarly, a correlation between (say) criminality and an authoritarian upbringing explains the former only through the implication that such an upbringing gives people motives to act criminally or weakens the motives for not doing so.

Causal adequacy and adequacy on the level of meaning

We have seen that correlations, even perfect correlations (corresponding to universal laws) are not *sufficient* to explain social facts. But are generalizations perhaps *necessary* for such explanations (despite being unnecessary, we have argued, for the explanation of human actions)? That is in fact the view of Max Weber.[57] According to Weber, social science explanation must satisfy a dual requirement: it must be both 'causally adequate' and 'adequate on the level of meaning'. Social science, for Weber, should explain phenomena in terms of theoretical ideal types, that is, theories describing a segment of social action on the assumption that it takes place in a certain institutional framework and is motivated by the pursuit of certain goals.[58] Such an explanation is 'adequate on the level of meaning' in that it displays the explanandum as the intelligible outcome of *motives*. And it will be 'causally adequate', if, 'according to established generalizations from experience', the occurrence of the explanandum was, in the existing circumstances, probable – that is, if there exists a *probabilistic law* to the effect that, in such circumstances, such a phenomenon usually occurs (no doubt a universal law would be still better, but can seldom be hoped for). In other words, explanation in terms of an ideal typical theory possesses causal adequacy to the extent that the theory corresponds to known facts.

An example, once again, may make this clearer. Weber himself cites explanation in terms of Gresham's Law, which states that 'bad money drives out good'; that is, if clipped or adulterated coins circulate along-side pure ones, the latter will disappear from circulation. This is derivable from an ideal typical economic theory which assumes that

[57] See his *The Theory of Social and Economic Organization*, pp. 95–100, 107–8.
[58] See above, pp. 58–60.

economic actors seek to maximize money gains; given that the defective coins command less confidence than the pure ones, people will then prefer to hold the latter and use the former for payments. There is, too, abundant evidence that the Law corresponds well to the facts. Now, suppose that in a particular community defective coins are circulating, and pure coins begin to disappear from circulation. We can explain the disappearance of the pure coins as due to the circulation of the defective ones, that is, in terms of Gresham's Law; and our explanation is adequate in both Weber's senses.

In view of our discussion of action-explanations, and the fact that Weber certainly thinks of social facts as complexes of actions, it may well be wondered why the meaningful adequacy of explanations should not be sufficient. Why is causal adequacy necessary? Weber's argument here seems to be in two stages. First, an explanation which is adequate only on the level of meaning, no matter how intelligible it renders the social fact to be explained, may always be mistaken – it is only, says Weber, a 'plausible hypothesis'. (It is, after all, easy to invent many plausible alternative hypothetical reasons and motives for an action.) It is necessary, therefore, to provide evidence that the motives and reasons attributed to actors are real rather than imaginary, and really explain their actions (we have seen that this can be difficult). Perhaps the best way to do it, Weber suggests, would be by applying psychological experimentation to the agents, but in social science this is practically never possible. Second, social science explains through ideal typical theories, that is, by attributing typical motives and so generating laws such as Gresham's Law and the other laws of economic theory. Hence, in social science, the appropriate method for verifying (or supporting) an explanatory attribution of reasons and motives is through an adequate correspondence of such theoretical laws to reality – that is, through causal adequacy. In other words, the role of causal adequacy is to provide evidence that a hypothetical 'meaningful explanation' is actually applicable to the case in question; and it is the method of doing so that is appropriate to social science.

Is Weber's argument correct? Let us apply it to an explanation of the disappearance of pure coins as due to the circulation of debased ones. Supposing that debased coins are indeed circulating in the community in question, this explanation *assumes* that people in that community have the typical motives of Gresham's Law. Does the fact that their behaviour conforms to an evidentially well-substantiated law confirm that assumption, and hence the correctness of the explanation? This is Weber's belief, but it is mistaken. There is no contradiction in asserting that bad money usually drives out good, that in a particular community on a particular occasion good money disappeared from circulation while bad money was circulating, yet on this occasion the disappearance of the good money was *not* due to the circulation of the bad. It is possible that the people in question did not act from the motives assumed by Gresham's Law, but from other motives and for a different reason. How people in general usually react to given circumstances is not compelling evidence as to the motives or reasons prompting the actions of a particular group of people in such circumstances on a particular occasion. If no other evidence is available, this information is not utterly valueless. But it certainly is not a necessary element in all social science explanations.

Nevertheless, while causal adequacy does not have the significance that Weber assigns to it, something not too unlike it can play a decisive role in the testing of a meaningful explanation. To illustrate this, let us consider another example, adapted from one discussed (for another purpose) by Robert Merton.[59] Suppose that in a particular community during a particular period the amount of borrowing from public libraries is abnormally high and so is the amount of unemployment. One might hypothesize that the high unemployment is the reason for the heavy borrowing, for (it may be supposed) unemployed men have more time and motivation to improve their skills, and books stocked in local libraries would be helpful to this end. This explanation is adequate on the level of meaning. According to Weber it should be checked by testing its causal adequacy, that is, by whether as a general rule increased unemployment coincides with increased borrowing from libraries, or in other words, by whether there is a correlation between the rate of unemployment and the rate of library borrowing in communities in general. But, as before, the existence or non-existence of this correlation of social facts provides information about how people generally behave, rather than about the reasons that explain the particular actions of particular people.

How might we go about looking for evidence as to the hypothesized reasons ? One way would be to look for a different sort of correlation; not a *general* correlation of *social* facts – of community unemployment rates and borrowing rates – but a *particular* correlation of *individual* facts. Did unemployed individuals in the community in question, during the period in question, borrow more books than employed individuals (after controlling for social class and other relevant variables) ? In other words, was there at that time a correlation between unemployment and borrowing at the individual level in the particular community ? This is a much more relevant test of our hypothetical explanation of the abnormally high rate of borrowing at that time than the existence or non-existence of any general correlation of unemployment rates and

[59] See R. Merton, *On Theoretical Sociology* (New York, Free Press, 1967), p. 148.

borrowing rates. If there is no such general correlation, but there was a correlation at the individual level as described, such a set of data supports rather than undermines the hypothesis that high unemployment was the reason for the heavy borrowing.

Notice, however, that even favourable correlations at the individual level would merely corroborate (in Popper's sense)[60] the original meaningful explanation, rather than definitively establish it. For not only might both the unemployment and the borrowing (so far as the correlations go) still be effects of some uncontrolled third factor; it could also be the case that, while unemployment was indeed one *reason* for book-borrowing, the *motives* from which the unemployed borrowed books was not that postulated in the explanatory hypothesis – perhaps they did so, not in order to improve their skills, but to kill time. Evidence as to motive would have to be sought in further details of the behaviour of the unemployed borrowers – for example, what *sort* of books they borrowed.

There is a further parallel between the evidential status of particular correlations at the individual level in relation to the explanation of social facts, and that of particular instances in relation to hypothetical universal laws; not only can appropriate correlations corroborate an explanation, their absence can falsify it. What is more, this may be so even if the hypothetical explanans (i.e. explanatory factor) really is the reason for some individual actions that are part of the social explanandum. For *it is necessary to distinguish between the reasons for individual actions and the reasons for the social fact itself*. To see this, suppose that, in the imaginary case we have been considering, there was no correlation between being unemployed and borrowing library books; but that some of the unemployed did borrow books and, furthermore, they assert in interviews that they largely did so because they were unemployed and had time to kill. The absence of the correlation does not show that they are mistaken or untruthful about their motives. It may be that, if the unemployed borrowers had not been unemployed, they would have borrowed fewer books, while other unemployed people, if they had not been unemployed, would have borrowed more. Unemployment may have affected different people differently – some read more to pass the time, some, perhaps, read less because anxiety interfered with their ability to concentrate – and hence have made no net difference to the rate of borrowing in the community. The absence of the appropriate particular correlation at the individual level shows that the social fact – the increased rate of borrowing – cannot be explained by the increased unemployment, though many individual acts of borrowing can be.

[60] See above, p. 18.

The Protestant ethic and the spirit of capitalism

It is of some interest to apply the present analysis to a celebrated explanation by Weber himself – that of the rise of modern capitalism in the West. Weber's thesis is that an important if not indispensable role was played by certain elements of the Protestant Reformation.[61] Specifically, the leaders of Calvinism and some other Protestant groups taught their followers that they must seek assurance as to their state of grace through ceaseless, systematic effort in an earthly calling. They must also abstain from self-indulgence and carnal pleasure. This way of life Weber dubbed 'inner-worldly asceticism' (meaning asceticism practised in the ordinary everyday world), and he believed it to be lacking in medieval Catholicism. His thesis holds that (given certain existing economic and other conditions) the adoption of this way of life by 'ascetic Protestants' promoted the accumulation of capital and hence economic growth. In other words, capitalistic behaviour was the outcome of certain religious motives. In corroboration of this thesis Weber pointed to rather rough correlations between 'ascetic Protestantism' and capitalistic development in the West.[62] In addition, he pointed out that in the highly developed civilizations of China, India, and Islam there was no significant development of an inner-worldly ascetic religious ethic, and also little or no development of capitalism of the Western type.[63]

Several commentators have suggested that Weber's studies of Eastern civilizations, interesting though they are in themselves, are not relevant to the validity of his explanation of the rise of modern *Western* capitalism.[64] This appears to be correct. Weber seems to have been trying to establish a perfect correlation, at the level of civilizations (or 'high civilizations'), between the existence of an influential religion incorporating an inner-worldly ascetic ethic, and the development of capitalism of the modern Western type. But if, in the Eastern civilizations, despite the absence of such a religion, capitalism had in fact arisen, this would not show that it would have done so in the West without such a religion. Nor would there be anything strange if people in different civilizations accumulated capital from different motives. Weber himself believed that in time the motives for capitalist behaviour

[61] See M. Weber, *The Protestant Ethic and the Spirit of Capitalism*, esp. chs IV and V.

[62] *Ibid.*, ch. I.

[63] For a convenient summary, see his *The Sociology of Religion* (London, Methuen Social Science Paperback, 1966), ch. XVI. His full-length studies are *The Religion of India* and *The Religion of China* (New York, Free Press, 1958 and 1951 respectively).

[64] E.g. A. MacIntyre, 'A Mistake about Causality in Social Science' in P. Laslett and W. G. Runciman (eds), *Philosophy, Politics and Society, Second Series* (Oxford, Blackwell, 1964), pp. 54–5.

even in the West ceased to be religious.[65] The later rise of capitalism in Catholic countries certainly does not disprove Weber's thesis.

Nevertheless, certain correlations *are* required by that thesis. To see their significance, let us distinguish two possible interpretations of the thesis, a stronger and a weaker. On the stronger interpretation, Weber holds the Protestant Reformation in its ascetic branches to be an *indispensable prerequisite* of the development of modern capitalism in the West on anything like its actual scale. This implies that, in the period of capitalist 'take-off', the great bulk of capitalistic producers either belonged to ascetic Protestant groups or at least were strongly influenced by them (e.g. as children of members). The weaker interpretation of Weber's thesis does not imply this, for it holds only that ascetic Protestantism *helped to foster* capitalism, made it develop faster and perhaps more widely than would otherwise have happened. But both versions imply a correlation at the individual level, in the West during the take-off period, between capitalistic activity and ascetic Protestant religious affiliation. Such a correlation would corroborate the hypothesis that ascetic Protestantism increased the *amount* of capitalist activity in the West during that period; its absence would falsify that hypothesis. Once again this is a separate question from the reasons and motives inspiring the behaviour of individual capitalists. For suppose that in the late medieval and early modern period, *both* Protestantism *and* Catholicism had preached an inner-worldly ascetic ethic which (though differing in specific content) equally led people to capitalistic behaviour. In that case, many Protestants would have been capitalists because of their Protestantism, in the sense that they behaved capitalistically in an attempt to achieve assurance as to their state of grace; yet there would be no correlation at the individual level between capitalism and Protestantism, and the Protestant Reformation would not have affected the level of capitalistic activity. If, on the other hand, the necessary correlation did exist, this would not of course prove Weber's thesis right; the causal connection between Protestantism and capitalism could have been in the opposite direction, as Marxists assert. To validate Weber, evidence is also required as to the motives from which capitalist producers behaved capitalistically, again drawn from further details of their behaviour.

Sociological explanation and historical explanation

It must be stressed that the correlations required to sustain explanations of some social facts are correlations between individual facts, not between social facts. The explanandum is thus not an *instance* of either of the sorts of facts whose correlation the explanation implies, and so it

---

[65] *The Protestant Ethic and the Spirit of Capitalism*, pp. 180–3.

is not explained by subsumption under a regularity. Of course, the explanation may *conform* to a generalization linking social facts, such as Gresham's Law. But since such a generalization is not required, a social fact is *never* explained *by* a generalization, even when it conforms to one. For Weber, as we have seen,[66] an explanation has to conform to such a generalization or else it is not a *sociological* (social scientific) explanation. In these terms, a social fact need not have a sociological explanation at all.

Weber also hints at a distinction between *sociological* and *historical* explanation of social facts, corresponding to a difference of scholarly perspective.[67] This idea is indeed quite popular. Both Isaiah Berlin[68] and William Dray,[69] for example, remark that the historian is not interested in the French Revolution simply as an instance of a revolution (that is, as an event sharing common characteristics with other revolutions), but wishes to explain it as a unique phenomenon, including those detailed characteristics which other revolutions do not manifest; it is the sociologist, they say, who is interested in the French Revolution simply as *a* revolution, in formulating laws relating to revolutions, and in explaining the French (or any other) revolution by its conformity to such a law.

Now, it is true enough that a given phenomenon can be described, and explained, in different degrees of detail. The French Revolution can be described as the violent overthrow of a ruling class (this, let us say, is the generic feature it shares with other revolutions); or it can be described as a series of events in which a popular assembly seized power from an absolute king, instituted a constitutional régime, abolished aristocratic privileges, later executed the king and established a nominally democratic republic, and so on and so on. The explanation of this series of events would certainly be different from an explanation conforming to a general law of revolutions. What must be rejected, however, is the suggestion of Dray and Berlin that the more detailed description excludes explanations conforming to general laws. No doubt the detailed description of the French Revolution describes a unique series of events, but no single event in the series need be considered unique; each can be described in terms of general categories (and is so described above) about which generalizations may hold. The truth appears to be, not that history and social science operate at different levels of detail and therefore explain in different ways, but

---

[66] Above, p. 100.

[67] See *The Theory of Social and Economic Organization*, pp. 96, 109.

[68] 'The Concept of Scientific History', in W. H. Dray (ed.), *Philosophical Analysis and History*, p. 31.

[69] W. H. Dray, *Laws and Explanation in History* (London, Oxford U.P., 1957), pp. 47–50.

that, at whatever level of detail a social phenomenon is investigated, the correct explanation may or may not conform to general laws.

Psychologism

We can now return to a question postponed earlier, that of the reduction of social science to psychology.[70] The view that this is possible has been attacked by Popper as 'psychologism', and it is also rejected not only by Durkheim but, perhaps more surprisingly, by Weber.[71] The reason, in Weber's case, is convincingly suggested by Parsons (and similar considerations certainly weigh with Durkheim and Popper too): 'psychology' is thought of as a body of propositions asserting universal traits of human nature, and thus incapable of explaining the particularity and diversity of social forms in different cultures.[72] Thus Popper berates John Stuart Mill for 'explaining' material progress – a culturally limited phenomenon – by an inherent and universal human desire for material comfort. In contrast to this stands Weber's explanation of the rise of modern capitalism (the main vehicle of material progress) in terms of motives arising from a specific socio-historical situation. Similarly, Durkheim castigates earlier sociologists for explaining religious institutions in terms of an innate human religious sentiment, family institutions in terms of innate sexual jealousy, filial piety, and paternal love, and so on. As Durkheim remarks, the sentiments that correspond to and uphold these institutions are as various as the forms they take, and are consequences of varying socialization. So, even if social facts are to be explained in terms of individuals' motives (as Weber would accept), these in turn are to be explained in terms of social facts, and so (it is asserted) social science cannot be reduced to psychology.

To be sure, the 'explanations' attacked by Durkheim and Popper are poor sociology. But this is not conclusive against psychologism, for they are equally poor psychology. It must be admitted that the relation between psychology and social science is different from that between, say, physics and biology. The reduction of biology to physics and chemistry would be a micro-reduction[73] that explained biological phenomena by considering biological organisms as made up of parts governed by the laws of physics and chemistry – laws which also apply to inorganic objects. In contrast, a science that seeks to explain the attitudes and behaviour of *individual* people has virtually no application

[70] See above, p. 83.
[71] See K. R. Popper, *The Poverty of Historicism*, pp. 152–9; E. Durkheim, *The Rules of Sociological Method*, pp. 97–112; M. Weber, *The Theory of Social and Economic Organization*, pp. 108–9.
[72] Introduction to *The Theory of Social and Economic Organization*, pp. 25–6.
[73] Cf. above, pp. 30–1.

to any 'object' (individual) that has not been crucially influenced by *social* relations and institutions. These relations and institutions never result from a coming together of unsocialized individuals. But this does not imply (as Popper believes)[74] that social science is irreducible to psychology. What it implies is that the variables of which *psychology* takes account must include the behaviour of other individuals. The psychological propositions in question will have, let us suppose, this general form: 'Given such-and-such a personal history, an individual (tends to) be actuated by such-and-such a motive' (say, the profit motive). That the history must include influences emanating from other individuals does not make this any the less a psychological proposition. In one way, too, the reduction of social science to such a psychology would seem to be a simpler matter than some of the scientific reductions already successfully carried out. The reduction of thermodynamics to mechanics required the discovery of *connecting laws* linking the concepts of the two sciences (e.g. temperature of a gas and mean kinetic energy of its molecules).[75] There would be no need for similar connecting laws to link social and psychological concepts, for (we have argued) social wholes and their characteristics simply *are* (or are deducible from) characteristics of related individuals.

According to Popper, however, it is not possible to derive explanations of social facts from psychological propositions of the kind suggested above.[76] He argues that, while the motives of individuals explain what they *attempt*, they cannot account for social *outcomes*, which result from complex and unforeseen interactions and reactions of many individuals, and hence rarely correspond to the intentions of any individual involved. The same set of motives can thus lead to quite different outcomes; for example, assuming the standard motives of buyers and sellers in a market (to buy cheap and sell dear), an increase in demand for a commodity can lead to either an increase or a decrease in its price (depending on whether the increased demand makes mass production possible).

This argument shows that motives *alone* do not explain social facts, and thus a psychology that explains motives would not, *alone*, do so. But it does not refute psychologism. No law or theory can *alone* explain a particular fact; a statement of the relevant *circumstances* is always necessary (cf. chapter 1).[77] And similarly in Popper's example, different outcomes are due to similar motives operating in different circumstances, i.e. different technical possibilities relating to mass production.

There seems to be no reason, *in principle*, why social science could

---

[74] Cf. his *The Open Society and its Enemies*, vol. 2, pp. 92–3.
[75] See above, p. 30.
[76] *The Open Society and its Enemies*, vol. 2, pp. 93–7.
[77] Pp. 21 ff. above.

not be reduced to the psychology we have been discussing. It is essential, however, to keep in mind Nagel's dictum that the reducibility of one science to another depends on the precise state of the sciences in question.[78] At the moment, a psychology capable of reducing the social sciences does not exist, and possibly it never will. Even if human motives never become explicable in terms of psychological laws, it remains the case that social facts can be explained according to the pattern outlined in this chapter, a pattern that differs markedly from that of physical explanation.

[78] Cf. p. 31 above.

CHAPTER 5

Functionalism and Explanation in Social Science

THE previous chapter considered explanation of social facts in relation to laws and generalizations, and to the intelligibility of action. I now wish to discuss the application to social science of so-called *functional* explanation. 'Functionalism' is an approach used in several social sciences, and 'function' is widely held to be an explanatory concept. This, however, is a controversial question and, as we shall see, a complex one. We must begin by making clear the meaning (or meanings) of 'function' and 'functionalism'.

Functionalism in biology
Functionalism in the social sciences rests on an analogy with biology, the science of organisms. These are entities with very special properties, which make the functionalist approach particularly suited to their study. In brief, they are *living systems*. As *systems*, they are wholes made up of interrelated parts; as *living* systems, they manifest certain characteristic activities of the organism as a whole and physiological processes carried on by its parts. These activities and processes enable the organism to persist as a unit over time, preserving its characteristic relation of parts and its characteristic activities and physiological processes – to remain, in other words, a living organism of a particular kind. Organisms are *self-maintaining* systems.

With reference to such a system, a part of it, or a process carried on within it, may be said to have a *function*. Thus, the heart in mammals (or the heart-*beat*) has the function of making the blood circulate; the circulation of the blood also has a function, or rather several functions, for example, to carry oxygen and nutrients to the tissues; and these processes too have a function. So also do activities of the organism itself, such as eating when hungry. The function of anything is always an *effect* which it achieves or makes possible when the organism is operating normally, but not just any effect – the heartbeat makes a particular sound as well as making the blood circulate, but the former is not its function.[1] A function is an effect that contributes to the self-maintenance of the organism, that is, helps it to survive. If any normal organic function ceases to be achieved, the organism will either die or at least its chances of survival will be reduced. The distinction between survival and death – between the maintenance and the destruction of the living organic system – is integral to the biological concept of function.

In the self-maintenance of living systems, an important role is played by the phenomenon of *homeostasis*. The life of many (perhaps all) organisms requires a considerable degree of constancy in features of the system which might, but for special mechanisms, vary greatly. A familiar example is the body temperature of mammals – human beings, for instance, cannot survive if their temperature varies much from $37°C$ ($98·6°F$). Mammals, then, need to (and do) incorporate homeostatic mechanisms which maintain body temperature at or near the appropriate level despite large changes in the temperature of the environment. This is achieved through processes of *negative feedback* – that is, processes that counteract any tendency to depart from the homeostatic norm. Raised temperature brings into play cooling processes such as sweating; lowered temperature, heat-producing processes such as shivering. Sweating and shivering thus have a homeostatic (more precisely, homoiothermic) function. Many biological functions are homeostatic functions.

Another important feature of living systems (organisms) is their *integrated* nature. The various processes and activities necessary to an organism's survival are not performed in mutual isolation; they are co-ordinated with one another and so to speak co-operate to maintain the life of the organism. This implies a mutual *adaptation* of the parts of any organism of a given sort. The human heart and lungs, for example, are so adapted to each other that they can interact to perform their various functions – the heart pumps the blood through the lungs where it is oxygenated, and thus oxygen is carried to the tissues. It would not be possible for, say, the heart of a fish to co-operate with human lungs in a human body to perform these functions – it is, rather,

[1] Cf. C. G. Hempel, 'The Logic of Functional Analysis', in L. Gross (ed.), *Symposium on Sociological Theory* (New York, Harper and Row, 1959), pp. 278–9. Notice, however, that the heart-sound may, according to some theories, have a biological function (cf. L. Salk, 'The Role of the Heartbeat in the Relations between Mother and Infant', *Scientific American*, May 1973, pp. 24–30). I am grateful to Gerald Lessnoff for this point.

adapted to the circulatory system of a fish, which has gills instead of lungs. The parts of an individual organism, and the processes they perform, are, we may say, *functionally related* to one another. But for this mutual adaptation, the organism could not survive, and so none of the physiological processes of its parts could be carried on. Thus there exists among the parts of an organism and the processes that they perform a relation of *mutual dependance and support* – each of these processes can go on only if other processes characteristic of the same organism go on too.

Functionalism in social science

Functionalist social scientists have been impressed by the analogies between biological organisms and societies. Societies, too, seem to be systems of interrelated, mutually dependent elements which co-operate (more or less) to preserve a recognizable whole which maintains itself over time. If this is so, some concepts of biology should be applicable in social science. One might, then, talk of the function of a social institution or organization, meaning thereby its contribution to the self-maintenance of the social system (society) to which it belongs. Admittedly, there are also disanalogies between societies and organisms. For many (not all) organisms, death is inevitable, whereas the social equivalent of death – the ceasing to exist of a society, in the sense that what was once a functioning society becomes no society at all – is relatively rare. This can of course occur if a society's members are wiped out by disease or war, but it is never inevitable. On the other hand, it can reasonably be presumed that all societies *would* 'die' unless certain activities were carried on within them – for example, activities to provide food for the population. One can, then, attempt to list the necessary conditions of societal viability, and to identify the contribution that various social activities make to fulfilling them (this is sometimes called 'requisite analysis').[2] The effect of a social activity in contributing to societal viability can then be called the 'social function' of the activity, analogously to biological functions.

But there is another important disanalogy between societies and organisms. Societies can, while more or less preserving their identity, change greatly in structure over time; whereas for mature biological organisms any considerable change means death or at least reduced viability – the only change possible is loss. An organism survives as the sort of organism it is, or not at all; a society can survive and yet become a quite different sort of society. Thus, the 'function' of a biological structure or process or behaviour pattern is a contribution to an

[2] See, for example, T. Parsons and N. J. Smelser, *Economy and Society* (New York, Free Press paperback, 1965), pp. 16 ff. and *passim*. Cf. also B. Malinowski, *op. cit.*, pp. 54 ff., 62–6, 125 and *passim*.

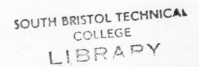

organism's survival as the sort of organism that it is – that is, as a particular sort of system of structures, processes, and characteristic behaviour patterns. But in relation to societies, what is necessary to preserve the system *in its existing form* has to be distinguished from what is necessary for the system to survive at all, *in any form whatever* – that is, from the general conditions of societal viability. Unless this distinction is clearly understood, the term 'social function' becomes ambiguous – it may refer to a contribution either to societal viability as such, or to the preservation of a particular sort of social system.

Of these two possible senses of 'social function' it is the latter only which, analogously to a biological function, implies a relation of adaptation between elements of the system. A particular sort of social system consists of particular sorts of social activities, institutions, etc. Thus, to say that a given institution contributes to maintaining a particular sort of society is to say that it contributes to maintaining the particular sorts of institutions, etc., of which the society consists. If several institutions coexisting in the same society are functional in this sense, they mutually maintain one another – are, in other words, mutually adapted. Such institutions may be said to have a *functional relation* to each other. (For example, it has been said that the nuclear family, which permits individual mobility, has such a relation to the industrial economy, which requires that mobility – whereas the extended family inhibits it).[3] I have elsewhere suggested[4] that the sort of functionalism which is concerned with the contributions of social institutions to maintaining a particular sort of social system, and therefore with the mutual adaptation of coexisting institutions in a society, should be called *institutional relation functionalism*; and that the sort of functionalism that is concerned with the conditions of survival of social systems as such, and the contributions of institutions to fulfilling them, should be called *societal survival functionalism*. That an institution has a societal survival function does not imply that it is better adapted to its coexisting institutions than to any others.

The fact that societies can change markedly while preserving their identity leads to a further important disanalogy between social and biological systems. Societies change in a gradual, piecemeal fashion, not all at once (even a 'revolution' cannot change everything simultaneously). Now, suppose that at a given moment a particular society's institutions are mutually well adapted and mutually sustaining (the society is 'functionally integrated'). Then, through growth of knowledge, the impingement of outside forces, or whatever, social change begins to

---

[3] Cf. T. Parsons, *Essays in Sociological Theory*, revised edn. (New York, Free Press paperback, 1964), p. 79.

[4] In my 'Functionalism and Explanation in Social Science', *Sociological Review*, new series, vol. 17 (1969), pp. 323–6.

occur. But since some institutions change before others, a mixture of old and new institutions comes to exist, which must be mutually less adapted than the original institutions. Coexisting institutions may even become mutually antagonistic rather than supportive (if, for example, industrialism spreads in a society with an extended family system). Such a situation is often described, in the functionalist perspective, as a *dysfunctional* relation between institutions, meaning that the co-existence of such institutions, instead of tending to persist because of their mutually supportive effect, sets up pressures for changes in one or the other or both. Equally, of course, coexisting institutions may have no effect whatever on one another's prospects of persistence. Again, relations between institutions need not be symmetrical: the effect of institution A on the persistence of institution B need not be the same as that of B on A. (In that case, sometimes one institution is rated as functional or dysfunctional from the standpoint of another, meaning that it tends to promote or hinder the latter's existence).[5] In most actual societies, no doubt, various combinations of these possible relations will hold between coexisting institutions at any moment.

The term 'dysfunctional', used above to describe a relation between institutions, is ambiguous in just the same way as 'functional'; in the context of societal survival, a dysfunctional institution or activity is one which makes that survival less likely (without, clearly, if it persists, actually ending society's existence). Examples might be modern war, or religions that discourage normal economic activity (as some have done). It is possible, too, that an institution could be in some aspects functional, and in others dysfunctional, in the societal survival sense.

The two functionalisms are not only distinguishable but separable also. Coexisting social practices may be interdependent and mutually sustaining, without in any way helping to fulfil the requirements of societal survival – they may even be *dys*functional in this sense. Thus Gunnar Myrdal, in *An American Dilemma*, suggested (very plausibly) the existence of what can be called a functional relation between discrimination by Whites against Negroes, and low Negro standards of living and conduct: discrimination made Negroes relatively poorer, less educated, more prone to crime, etc.; and these facts in turn made Whites discriminate against them.[6] Yet discrimination and low standards are not helpful to societal survival – if anything the reverse.

---

[5] Examples of this usage can be found in D. Apter, *The Politics of Modernization* (Chicago U.P., 1965), pp. 68, 257, 288, 308; and in R. E. Jones, *The Functional Analysis of Politics* (London, Routledge and Kegan Paul, 1967), p. 85, who follows Gabriel Almond.

[6] See G. Myrdal, *Value in Social Theory* (London, Routledge and Kegan Paul, 1958), p. 188.

H

Societal survival functionalism and institutional relation functionalism
In discussing the relevance of functionalism to explaining why social phenomena are what they are (which is the main task of this chapter) it will be essential to distinguish clearly the two different sorts of functionalism defined above. Some writers have indeed noted this distinction,[7] but very many have confused the two (one at least has done both)[8] or expressed themselves ambiguously. Nor is ambiguity on this point avoided by distinguishing, as some sociologists have,[9] between a functionalism concerned with the relation of parts of society to each other and a functionalism concerned with the relation of parts of society to society as a whole; 'society as a whole' could refer to either a particular social system or any social system whatever (if the former, these two functionalisms are essentially identical – both are institutional relation functionalism; if the latter, the second of them *might* be equivalent to societal survival functionalism).

The same ambiguity lurks in the account given by the pioneer functionalist Radcliffe-Brown, who defines the social function of an institution as the correspondence between it and the necessary conditions of existence of 'the social organism'.[10] Later in the same essay he says that the function of 'any recurrent activity' is its contribution to maintaining the 'structural continuity',[11] which seems to mean the persistence of a particular sort of social system and suggests he has institutional relation functionalism in mind; but he also says that a society can change its 'structural type' without breach of continuity,[1] so perhaps 'continuity' means societal survival as such. Most probably, Radcliffe-Brown was not clearly aware that two different conceptions are possible. He argues that *religions* have the function of maintaining in people's minds the sentiments on which their society's existence depends, and hence there is covariation between religions and other elements of the social system – for example, in warlike societies, religion instils sentiments of patriotism and devotion in battle.[13] This is clearly institutional relation functionalism. Yet Radcliffe-Brown concludes his argument by asserting that religion's social function is

[7] For example, P. S. Cohen, *op. cit.*, pp. 61–2.

[8] Robert Merton, *op. cit.*, distinguishes between functional analysis as 'establishing empirical interrelations between "parts" of a social system', and as 'showing the "value for society" of a socially standardized practice or a social organization' (p. 103) – a distinction similar to my own. But he also confuses the two conceptions – see, for example, p. 116 below.

[9] For example, K. Davis, 'The Myth of Functional Analysis as a Special Method in Sociology and Anthropology', *American Sociological Review*, vol. 24 (1959), pp. 758–9; G. C. Homans, *Sentiments and Activities* (London, Routledge and Kegan Paul, 1962), pp. 23–4.

[10] A. R. Radcliffe-Brown, *Structure and Function in Primitive Society* (London, Cohen and West, 1952), p. 178.

[11] *Ibid.*, p. 180.   [12] *Ibid.*, p. 181.   [13] *Ibid.*, pp. 157–63.

above all to develop in mankind that sense of dependence which is essential to social life[14] – and this, just as plainly, is societal survival functionalism.

Similar ambiguity and uncertainty is to be found in the writings of Radcliffe-Brown's contemporary and fellow-functionalist, Malinowski. For Malinowski, the function of an item of 'culture' (roughly, a social practice) is its role in fulfilling some biological or psychological need of individuals, rather than the necessary conditions of existence of social systems as such.[15] But he points out that no culture (society) can exist unless it provides for these individual needs, so this conception of 'function' is also a societal survival one. At the same time, Malinowski remarks that the concept of function shows us that an institution is dependent on 'the total character of a culture', and that culture is a whole in which the various elements are interdependent.[16] This is, of course, institutional relation functionalism.

Confusion between the two sorts of functionalism appears rather frequently in relation to social change. Thus John Rex, discussing Radcliffe-Brown's idea that a society may change its 'structural type' (that is, evolve from one well-adjusted system of institutions to another), suggests that the criteria for identifying such an event include extensive instability (that is, disorder) in a previously stable community.[17] Now, evolution from one structural type to another would at an intermediate stage involve a *dysfunctional relation* between institutions, that is, a combination of institutions that tends not to persist. But there is no necessity for such an evolution to produce disorder, which is dysfunctional in a societal survival sense. It might be argued that a dysfunctional relation between institutions must also be dysfunctional in the societal survival sense, in that a lack of mutual adaptation among a society's institutions will make for breakdown and even violent conflict. (This seems, indeed, to be Radcliffe-Brown's view.)[18] It would then follow that social change is dysfunctional in the societal survival sense whenever it disturbs mutually adapted institutions. But while this may quite often be true, especially if the change in question is major, rapid, or opposed by vested interests, it is important to stress that any association between the two sorts of dysfunction is a matter of contingent fact, not conceptual identity. Peaceful transformation of a previously stable society is not a logical contradiction or even a practical impossibility.

[14] A. R. Radcliffe-Brown, *Structure and Function in Primitive Society*, pp. 175-7.
[15] B. Malinowski, *op. cit.*, pp. 37-9.   [16] *Ibid.*, pp. 50 and 150.
[17] J. Rex, *Key Problems of Sociological Theory* (London, Routledge and Kegan Paul paperback, 1970), pp. 70-2.
[18] See A. R. Radcliffe-Brown, *op. cit.*, pp. 182-4.

Just as the coexistence of mutually ill-adapted institutions (such as the industrial economy and the extended family) does not necessarily imply disorder or violence, violence itself may actually have a mutually sustaining (functional) relationship with other social institutions in a persisting social system. According to Gluckman, violent rebellion had such a relation to the political institutions of some African societies; not only did the political institutions provoke rebellions, rebellions, by acting as a safety-valve, helped to preserve the political institutions in their existing form.[19] It remains true that social violence is, in the societal survival sense, dysfunctional. Changes in either of these mutually well-adapted institutions would therefore be, in that sense, functional rather than dysfunctional. The same is true in regard to White discrimination against Negroes, and low Negro standards of living and conduct, which, if Myrdal's account is correct, are functionally related.[20]

Confusion in relation to the functional significance of change is also manifested by another prominent functionalist sociologist, Talcott Parsons. For Parsons, the functional relevance of a process is its consequences for the system 'in terms of maintenance of stability or production of change, of integration or disruption of the system'.[21] Here 'change' and 'disruption' are apparently identified, and opposed to 'stability' and 'integration'. We have seen that identification of change and disruption would naturally result from confusing the two functionalisms. The word 'stability' is, interestingly, ambiguous in a way that parallels the ambiguity of 'social function': that is, it can, in everyday usage, mean the absence of either change or disorder. (Curiously, '*instability*' seems always to signify disorder). This ambiguity is reflected in Parsons's definition of function, and possibly led him into confusion.

There is a similar ambiguity, too, in the term 'integration', at any rate in sociological usage, as is apparent in Parsons's definition. It crops up again in the work of another famous functionalist sociologist, Robert Merton. In one place Merton writes: 'Most societies are integrated to the extent that many, if not all, of their several elements are reciprocally adjusted. [They] do not have a random assortment of attributes, but these are variously interconnected and often mutually sustaining.'[22] Here, 'integration' clearly means a functional relation of institutions. But elsewhere Merton identifies integration with social *solidarity*, i.e. co-operation and absence of conflict,[23] which is an important function

[19] M. Gluckman, *Custom and Conflict in Africa* (Oxford, Blackwell, 1956), pp. 27–53.
[20] See above, p 113.
[21] *The Social System* (New York, Free Press paperback, 1964), pp. 21–2.
[22] *Op. cit.*, p. 95.   [23] *Ibid.*, pp. 80–3.

in the societal survival sense. There is a strong hint, also, of a similar confusion in Merton's handling of the concept of 'dysfunction' (which he in fact originated). Social change, says Merton, results from the stresses and strains and eventual institutional breakdowns that result from social dysfunctions.[24] Now, dysfunctional relations between institutions by definition lead to institutional change, but not necessarily via breakdowns, which are dysfunctions in the societal survival sense. Breakdowns may indeed lead to changes, but are not required for them (just as, we saw, changes may lead to breakdowns, but need not).

A conceptual connection between the two functionalisms
Despite the indubitable conceptual distinctness of the two sorts of functionalism, there nevertheless exists, in one particular sort of case, a conceptual connection between them. Consider, for example, the usual analysis of institutionalized joking and avoidance relations in tribal societies, according to which they have the function of forestalling otherwise likely social conflicts.[25] At first, perhaps, this appears to attribute a societal survival function to these institutions, that of maintaining order. But the appearance is deceptive. Avoidance and joking relations between given categories of persons have the effect described only in a particular kind of society, namely, societies whose structure is such as to produce a high risk of conflict between these persons and in which social order would be endangered by such conflict. An example is Tallensi society, in which, according to Goldschmidt, there is a lineage system that creates potential tension between fathers and sons, which is forestalled by mutual avoidance.[26] This avoidance relation neutralizes potentially *dysfunctional* consequences (in the societal survival sense) of the Tallensi lineage system; thus it increases the viability of the *particular institutions* that constitute the Tallensi social system, in particular its lineage system. What the functional analysis asserts is a relation of dependence between institutions – the dependence of the Tallensi lineage system and perhaps other Tallensi institutions on father-son avoidance – rather than that the survival of society as such depends on avoidance institutions. What is involved is thus a functional relation between institutions, in which one institution offsets another's potential dysfunctional consequences for societal survival.

This kind of functionalist analysis is far from rare. Another example is the Marxist theory of the state, according to which the state is needed to control the conflict engendered by the class-system, and thus helps

---

²⁴ *Op. cit.*, pp. 94–5, 107.
²⁵ Cf. A. R. Radcliffe-Brown, *op. cit.*, ch. V.
²⁶ W. Goldschmidt, *Comparative Functionalism* (Berkeley, University of California Press, 1966), pp. 72–5.

to preserve the class-system. Yet another instance is Gellner's account of Berber beliefs about a notable called the *agurram*, who mediates between feuding tribes and who, the tribesmen say, is chosen by God, though in fact they choose him themselves.[27] This belief enables the tribesmen to accept the *agurram's* decision and thus helps to preserve peace, whereas Berber values would preclude as weakness their acceptance of decisions of an arbitrator acknowledged to be humanly appointed. Thus, the Berber belief in divine selection of the *agurram* makes their value-system more viable than it would otherwise be.

Functional explanation

Functionalism in social science is not simply a matter of describing the functions of social phenomena. Most functionalists have believed that, in showing some item to have a social function, they have explained its existence. According to Malinowski, for example, functionalism 'aims at the explanation of anthropological facts at all levels of development by their function'.[28] Even a writer generally critical of functionalism, John Rex, agrees that activities that do have the task of maintaining the social structure (that is, that perform a social function) are thereby explained.[29] Yet the explanatory value of functionalism is a controversial question, to which we must now turn. If there are indeed two functionalisms rather than one, we must obviously consider them separately. Let us first, then, consider whether the fact that an item has a function in the societal survival sense explains why it exists.

In earlier chapters, we looked at two distinct sorts of explanation of particular facts, namely, explanation of human actions in terms of the agent's motives and reasons for acting, and of other phenomena by pointing out their cause in the Humean sense.[30] Different as these two sorts of explanation are, causes, reasons, and motives are all alike in that they exist *antecedent* to the explanandum; a feature which, indeed, seems to be necessary to their capacity to explain. But the contribution of a social item to societal survival clearly cannot exist prior to that item's existence. How then can it explain it?

Since the explanation of a social fact, we saw, needs to be intelligible in terms of the reasons and motives of the people involved, any vindication of the explanatory capacity of societal survival functionalism must show how this would be the case in such an explanation. It is, of course, possible that people might be aware that a social practice contributes to societal survival, and perform it because they wish its function to be fulfilled. But then the explanation, strictly speaking, is not the function

---

[27] E. Gellner, 'Concepts and Society', in B. R. Wilson (ed.), *Rationality*, pp. 43–5.
[28] Quoted in R. Merton, *op. cit.*, p. 76.   [29] *Op. cit.*, p. 65.
[30] See above, pp. 83–92 and 21–7 respectively.

but the desire to realize it. And such an explanation does not even imply that the practice has any function – only that the people involved *believe* that it has. In order to assimilate functional explanation of the societal survival sort to explanation in terms of reasons and motives, it would be necessary to assume that, *in general*, when a practice has such a function the people involved know this, and participate in it for the sake of its function. A reference to the function could then be understood as a shorthand reference to this motive. But unfortunately the assumption is highly implausible, for it greatly overrates the average person's sociological knowledge. It might perhaps be argued that this is irrelevant because it is not people in general who determine social institutions, but rather powerful minorities. But even if this is true, it is not a very plausible assumption that the latter deliberately sustain practices for the sake of their societal survival functions, or even, as a rule, know what these are. (Even sociologists are not agreed on this.)[31] Thus, a mere reference to a societal survival function is not equivalent to a motive explanation, even if in a particular case the appropriate motive happens to be operative, because there is no license to infer the motive from the function. It is necessary to state such a motive explicitly.

Many functionalists, in any case, have no wish to assimilate functional explanations to motive explanations – quite the reverse. Kingsley Davis, for example, remarks that the functional theory of incest taboos or magical practices does *not* hold that these practices exist because their function is perceived – the participants' purposes may be quite different.[32] Malinowski contrasts the function of an institution with its 'charter', that is, the idea of it entertained by members of the community.[33] Merton, again, distinguishes 'manifest' from 'latent' functions, the former being functions which are 'intended and recognized by participants in the system', whereas the latter are not.[34] There is no doubt that he thinks that the latent functions of practices serve to explain their existence just as much as manifest functions; for example, a practice that fails to achieve its explicit purpose (such as rain ceremonials of primitive societies) should often be attributed to its latent functions, rather than just to ignorance, superstition, or inertia.[35]

But even if participants in a practice have no inkling of its function, could we not assimilate this kind of functional explanation to motive explanation by distinguishing between the *origin* of a practice, and its *persistence*? That an existing practice continues to exist, it might be argued, scarcely requires any explanation beyond habit and inertia; but the origin of practices is a different matter. Is it not plausible to

---

[31] Cf. the argument of G. C. Homans, *Sentiments and Activities*, pp. 27–8.
[32] *Op. cit.*, p. 765.   [33] B. Malinowski, *op. cit.*, pp. 48, 53.
[34] R. Merton, *op. cit.*, p. 105.   [35] *Ibid.*, p. 118.

suppose that a practice might originate through appreciation of its function, but that this motive should eventually be forgotten? In that case, it would be reasonable to say that the function explains the practice's existence. And no doubt there are such cases. However, for reasons already mentioned, there is no good reason to suppose that whenever a practice has a societal survival function it originated in this way. This can be illustrated by a familiar theory which makes such a supposition; the so-called theory of social contract explains the origin of government in terms of an appreciation of its societal survival function – namely, the maintenance of peace and security – by men living in a 'state of nature'. But this is not a very plausible theory. Much more likely is that government owes its origin to the desire of some individuals (who became rulers) for power and self-aggrandizement, and to their ability to achieve this goal.

Natural selection

We saw earlier that functionalism in social science rests on an analogy with biology. In biology, furthermore, the attribution of a survival function ('survival value') to an anatomical structure or physiological process or behavioural trait *is* normally acceptable as an explanation of why it is found. We must now consider what the rationale behind this is, and whether it is applicable in social science too. First of all, survival value does not explain the *origin* of a biological item. The origin of new structures and processes in biological organisms is to be explained in terms of laws governing recombination of genetic material, genetic mutations, and the phenotypic expression of genes. But the fact that a new biological item makes its appearance in a population of organisms does not mean that it will *survive*. Most genetic novelties are harmful, that is, dysfunctional in the survival sense, and quickly disappear. The Darwinian struggle for existence ensures that most organisms die quite quickly and without reproducing themselves. Those that survive are 'the fittest' – that is, those possessing the most functional traits, in the survival sense. Thus, it can be expected that few dysfunctional traits will survive in biological organisms, and that the vast majority of existing traits are functional in the survival sense. To point out the 'survival value' of a biological trait is therefore to indicate something without which it probably would not have survived, and so, in a very general way, to explain its survival.

This kind of argument is not, however, applicable to the social context. There is no 'struggle for survival' between societies to ensure that the vast majority of social practices are functional in the survival sense. There are, it is true, wars between societies which sometimes lead to the elimination of institutions in the defeated society. But there is no particular reason why such institutions should be dysfunctional;

they are likely, rather, to be institutions which the conquerors dislike – possibly from moral motives, possibly because they perceive them as a threat – and therefore destroy. Only if conquerors were generally motivated by a desire to root out dysfunctional institutions, and knew which these were, would war have an effect at all analogous to Darwinian natural selection. However, there are a few limited areas in which a social analogue of Darwinian selection does operate. One sometimes cited is competition between firms in a free market.[36] Firms are social systems which (unlike whole societies) frequently perish through failure in a competitive process. If the market works efficiently, it should tend to eliminate firms that have inefficient characteristics, inefficiency being, in this context, dysfunctional in the survival sense. The persistence of some characteristic of firms could then be explained by pointing out in what way it promotes their efficiency, even if the people involved were unaware of the fact (which is perhaps not very likely). But it seems to be rare for competition in the market to be sufficiently intense to make the analogy with natural selection a strong one. Very many inefficient practices seem to survive.

Reverting to wider social systems, is there any process which substitutes for Darwinian-type selection and brings it about that the great majority of practices are functional in the societal survival sense? We have already rejected the notion that the motives of those who establish and participate in social practices could do so. However, it has been pointed out by several writers[37] that if a society fails to provide what is necessary for the survival of its members (and therefore of itself) it will quickly cease to exist, regardless of competition with other societies. This is true, but it does not ensure that dysfunctional practices cease to exist, much less items which are neither functional nor dysfunctional but simply neutral. Very severely dysfunctional practices – those that are *lethal* to societal survival – will of course disappear, either by destroying their societies or through deliberate abandonment.[38] But this is perfectly compatible with the persistence of many (even a majority of) dysfunctional and neutral practices. Thus, to point out that some practice has a particular societal survival function is *not* to indicate something but for which it probably would not have survived.

Is it not, however, to indicate something which *improves* its chance of survival? It might seem that, since a practice's societal survival

---

[36] Cf. P. S. Cohen, *op. cit.*, p. 50; A. L. Stinchcombe, *Constructing Social Theories* (New York, Harcourt, Brace and World, 1968), p. 85.

[37] E.g. B. Malinowski, *op. cit.*, pp. 143–4; cf. B. F. Skinner, *op. cit.*, pp. 129, 133.

[38] Cf. the argument of R. Needham, *Structure and Sentiment* (Chicago U.P., 1962), pp. 115–16, on the elimination of grossly inefficient institutions by deliberate abandonment.

function, by definition, makes the survival of the society to which the practice belongs more likely than would otherwise be the case (other things equal), it must also make the survival of the practice itself more likely than if the latter had no societal survival function. This is, indeed, true. However, the function equally improves the prospects for survival of all *other* practices, institutions, etc., belonging to the same society, whether they are functional in this sense or not. It is therefore as relevant to the explanation of *their* survival, as to that of the practice that fulfils the function. It is not the case, as many functionalists have supposed, that the societal survival function of a practice is peculiarly relevant to explaining the survival of that practice itself.

Essential functions

The next stage of our discussion requires a distinction between social items which are *essential* to societal survival (for example, a system for distributing food to the population), and those which simply *enhance* the viability of any society which happens to possess them (such as an efficient medical service).

According to an argument of Carl Hempel, functional explanation is valid if and only if it shows that some item is essential to the functioning of the system to which it belongs.[39] In that case, it is possible to construct a deductive argument like the following:

Major premise: System S functions only if item i is present in S.

Minor premise: At time t, system S functions.

Conclusion: At time t, item i is present in S.

If for 'system S' we substitute 'a society', understand 'functions' as equivalent to 'exists' or 'survives', and add 'place p' to 'time t', we get:

Major premise: A society exists only if item i is present in it.

Minor premise: A society exists in place p at time t.

Conclusion: Item i is present in the society existing in place p at time t.

In other words, from the fact that some item is a necessary condition of existence of a society, plus the fact that a particular society exists, we can deduce that the item is present in that society (for example, that a

[39] 'The Logic of Functional Analysis' in L. Gross (ed.), *Symposium on Sociological Theory*, pp. 283–4.

food distribution system is present in British society). This means, according to Hempel, that the two premises explain why the item is present.

But this argument seems to be based on the fallacious belief that to deduce the existence of something from true premises is necessarily to explain it. Its fallaciousness is easily shown. We saw in chapter 1[40] that if a cause is the necessary and sufficient condition of its effect, the effect is also the necessary and sufficient condition of its cause. This makes it possible to deduce the occurrence of the cause from that of the effect. But it would be exceedingly strange to say that the cause is explained by its effect.

An example may make this clearer. Suppose that, in certain circumstances, water boils if and only if its temperature rises to 100°C; and that some water, in those circumstances, rose to 100°C and boiled. We can now construct this deduction:

Major premise: Water in circumstances X boils only if its temperature rises to 100°C.

Minor premise: Some water, in circumstances X, boiled.

Conclusion: The water's temperature rose to 100°C.

The premises, if true, guarantee the truth of the conclusion, but they do not *explain* the fact it expresses. The water did not rise in temperature because it boiled, but the other way round. And this example is exactly parallel to Hempel's argument, in which the existence of an item is deduced from that of something for whose existence it is necessary. That argument, therefore, does not show that the necessity of an item to societal survival explains its existence.[41]

But it does not follow that it is not explanatory at all. What *can* be explained by showing some item to be essential to societal survival is a universal sociological law (if there are any). Suppose that (as many functionalists believe), the following law is true: 'All societies are stratified' (that is, in all societies individuals are unequal in wealth and status).[42] The standard functionalist explanation of this is approximately as follows. All societies have some division of labour, that is, their members occupy different social roles. The performance of some roles is both relatively onerous, and essential to societal survival. Individuals will be unwilling to perform these roles unless they receive

[40] Above, p. 23.
[41] Ernest Nagel's well-known account of teleological explanation (*op. cit.*, pp. 400–22) is, I believe, vitiated by similar considerations.
[42] See footnote 25 to ch. 2 above.

in return more wealth and/or status than occupants of other roles. Thus no society can survive unless it rewards some of its members more than others. Hence all (surviving) societies are stratified. That is, all societies are stratified because stratification is essential to societal survival. But this no more explains why in a particular society – say, *in British society now* – there is stratification, than the theory of change of physical state, which explains why (under certain conditions) no water boils unless its temperature reaches 100°C, can explain why the temperature of some particular water boiling under these conditions reached 100°C.

How is it that the functionalist theory can explain a law, but not particular cases subsumed by the law? The reason is that the theory shows why, *if any society exists*, it is stratified;[43] and this is what the law 'All societies are stratified' actually asserts. It does not assert or imply that any stratified society exists. By contrast, a particular statement such as 'British society now, is stratified' does assert the existence of a stratified society, and therefore neither the theory nor the law suffices to explain the fact. A law can of course explain a particular fact when combined with a suitable particular premise (as explained in chapter 1). But the functionalist theory fails to provide the latter.

To put it another way: a Hempel-type functionalist deduction can show (assuming its assertions to be true) that, if a society has survived it must be stratified; it does not show what made it, or makes it, stratified. *It thus does not show why stratification exists.* From the fact that an unstratified society is an impossibility, it does not follow that social stratification ever exists anywhere – there may be no social stratification, and hence no societies (and presumably no men either). An explanation of the existence of stratification must show why this is not the case. I suggest that this explanation requires an account of the facts of human psychology and behaviour that lead to the stratification: for example, that the people involved seek wealth and status for themselves and their children and have unequal abilities; hence different people have unequal amounts of wealth and status. Let us assume, for simplicity, that this makes *all* societies stratified. Then, these facts of human psychology and behaviour ('human nature') would also explain *why* all societies are stratified. In other words, there are two different possible kinds of explanation of this law: one (psycho-behavioural) which refers to traits of human nature which bring about certain consequences in all societies; and one (functional) which refers to the necessity of a given characteristic if any social system is to exist. But only the psycho-behavioural explanation can explain why that characteristic exists (by showing it to be the consequence of traits of human nature); and only the psycho-behavioural explanation explains why all

[43] I am grateful to Mary Haight for pointing this out to me.

societies have the characteristic by specifying the antecedent facts of which the characteristic is a result.

To avoid misunderstanding, it should be stressed that the two possible kinds of explanation (psycho-behavioural and functional) of a law such as 'all societies are stratified' are not *alternative* explanations in the sense that if one is correct the other cannot be. It is in principle possible that the functionalist theory of stratification is correct, and that universal stratification is also the outcome of human nature (that is, of universal self-seeking combined with unequal ability). It is equally possible that the latter is the case, but the former is not – in which case human nature is the only explanation of the law. (Presumably every such law has its explanation in human nature). It is also possible in principle (though not in reality) that the functionalist theory might be correct, but that human nature might fail to bring stratification about, or even prevent it. For example, people might find it insupportable that anyone else should be richer, and be able (through political action) to enforce economic equality. Egalitarian sentiment might also bring about equality of status. In that case, according to the functionalist theory, the onerous tasks on which societal survival depends would not be adequately performed, and society would perish – in which case, there would be no functionalist (or any other) theory of stratification.

Institutional relation functionalism and explanation

What, now, of the explanatory force of institutional relation functionalism? We must distinguish two forms of this: *unidirectional*, where one institution is 'functional for' another or others, i.e. favours the latter's development or persistence; and *reciprocal*, where each of two institutions is 'functional for' (favours) the other. The unidirectional form cannot explain why the functional institution exists. It certainly does not explain its existence by its function, which is to favour the existence of *another* institution or institutions (as, a Marxist might say, the function of the State is to preserve class divisions). Of course, if the State is a necessary condition for the preservation of class divisions, this would explain why the State is always present when class divisions are present; but it would not explain why existing States exist (for there might be no state and no class divisions, as indeed Marxists aver is possible – explaining their presence or absence in given societies in terms of the stage of evolution reached by the forces of production). It could be, of course, that the ruling class deliberately maintains the State in order to preserve the class structure; but then the explanation of the State's existence would be the motives of the ruling class and its power derived from control of the forces of production, rather than the function of the State as such.

The reciprocal form of institutional relation functionalism, however, does have explanatory power. Consider the relation which, it has been suggested, exists between the nuclear family and industrialism: the nuclear family, unlike other family systems, is compatible with the individual social mobility that industrialism requires.[44] Thus in the USA, for example, where both are found, the existence of an industrial economy is partly explained by the nuclear family system; and, conversely, the industrial economy, in bringing about individual mobility, which is incompatible with other family systems, partly explains the existence of the nuclear family system. In other words, where a reciprocal functional relation is demonstrated between two coexisting institutions, A and B, each is at least partially explained. Furthermore, each is explained *by its function*; for the function of A is to promote B and B in turn promotes A – so A's function favours A's own existence. (Similarly, *mutatis mutandis*, with B's function.) And here there is no dichotomy of functional and psycho-behavioural explanations; if the nuclear family promotes industrialism, it promotes behaviour that results in industrialism, and if industrialism promotes the nuclear family, it promotes behaviour of which the nuclear family is the result.

But does this analysis reveal a real difference between the two functionalisms in relation to explanation? It might be argued that it is possible to apply a similar analysis to societal survival functionalism, as follows. If more than one type of institution is necessary to societal survival (as is supposed by the 'requisite analysts', and is plausible enough), there must be a relation of mutual support between them. Consider the relation between the economy and the State, on the assumption that the former performs the essential function of food provision, and the latter the essential function of maintaining order. Given these assumptions, economic activity could not take place but for the State, nor the State exist without economic activity: State and economy are each a necessary condition of the other, and the existence of each is therefore necessary to the explanation of the other's existence. (This, by the way, is *not* a case of reciprocal institutional relation functionalism, which refers to a mutual *adaptation* of institutions, such that each favours the other as against alternative forms. The relation between State and economy described here implies nothing about what forms of economy and State are well adapted to each other).

This argument appears to be correct so far as it goes, but it does not show that either State or economy is explained *by its function* – for the function of each is to fulfil a necessary condition of existence, not of the other specifically, but of social life as such. Only if every item of social life fulfilled a necessary condition of existence of the State, would the State's societal survival function be involved in the explanation of its

---

[44] Cf. footnote 3 to this chapter.

own existence. But this is not the case – some social items are even dysfunctional in the societal survival sense. And of course, the mere fact that an institution has a societal survival function does not in itself imply that any other institution has such a function, and so does not imply any relation of reciprocal support.

Teleological explanation

Before concluding this chapter, we should consider a kind of explanation often thought to be germane to its theme, namely *teleological explanation*. The relevant sense of this rather ambiguous expression is most easily expounded in relation to biology. Biological organisms, as we saw earlier,[45] are systems which tend to preserve a rough constancy in certain of their features, thanks to mechanisms (called 'homeostatic') which counteract incipient deviations from the norm. This fact can be expressed in *teleological laws*,[46] such as: 'Human beings (tend to) maintain a body temperature of about 37°C'. In this connection, the idea of teleological explanation is that such laws, which express the tendency of a system to maintain a so-called *goal-state*, explain operations which help to maintain that State. Thus, if one were to ask why human beings shiver and sweat, the teleological explanation would be that they do so *in order to* maintain the normal body temperature of 37°C. The phrase 'in order to' does not here imply purpose, only that the organism is so constituted that it does tend to maintain the normal body temperature, by means of various mechanisms including sweating and shivering. Clearly teleological explanation departs markedly from the explanatory patterns discussed so far: the explanandum is explained, not by any antecedent, but by its consequence, the goal-state. Roughly, the explanation says that human beings shiver and sweat *because* shivering and sweating tend to maintain the normal body temperature.

Teleogical explanation in biology is explanation in terms of function – the maintenance of the normal body temperature is the *function* of both sweating and shivering. Two questions arise: is this a valid form of explanation? and does it find parallel application in social science? I believe not, in both cases. But it suffices that the answer to one of these questions be negative, to show that teleological explanation cannot explain social facts.

As regards the validity of teleological explanation, it at once seems odd to offer teleological explanations of such phenomena as sweating and shivering, since they can be explained *causally* through non-teleological laws: a slight fall in body temperature below the norm causes physiological changes which in turn cause shivering, and correspondingly with sweating. If the causal explanations are correct, it is

[45] Above, p. 110.   [46] Cf. A. Ryan, *op. cit.*, p. 184.

hard to see how or in what sense quite different teleological explanations of the same explananda can be correct too. It is essential here to distinguish the question of the validity of teleological explanation from that of the genuineness of teleological laws. These laws certainly apply to biological organisms, but it does not follow that teleological explanations are valid. The relation between laws and explanation is quite specific (and is set out in chapter I).[47] Teleological 'explanation' does not conform to it.

It might be argued, in reply, that there are some facts that cannot be explained causally, and that teleological explanations of such facts can therefore be given, which are not in conflict with causal explanations. One can explain causally what makes the human organism shiver, what makes it sweat, and so on; but it is another question why the human organism possesses a whole battery of co-ordinated mechanisms, including shivering and sweating, which act together so that its temperature remains close to 37°C. Each of the mechanisms can, *singly*, presumably be explained in terms of biological evolution. But why should all of these mechanisms have developed *together* in such a way as to complement each other in bringing about the result that they do? The *survival* of such functional complexes can be explained by natural selection, for they have great survival value; but natural selection cannot explain the *origin* of anything. Could they have come into existence by chance? If this seems unlikely, and yet no causal explanation can be given of their existence, there is an explanatory lacuna which, it might be argued, teleological explanation can fill.[48]

However, even if it were true that no causal account can explain these facts, it would not follow that they could be explained teleologically. The shortcomings of teleological explanation remain. It is not easy to make sense of the idea that the existence of the complex of homoiothermic mechanisms in the human body, and of the various co-ordinated activities it carries on, are explained by the effect of these activities, i.e. the constant temperature of the human body (unless one supposes that Providence or some such force assembled the complex in order to realize the effect). Nor is it clear that a causal explanation of such phenomena is in principle impossible. The relevant antecedent facts are unknown and perhaps unknowable, but if they were known they might permit a causal account of the evolution of the phenomena in question.

---

[47] See pp. 21–8 above.

[48] Cf. W. W. Isajiw, *Causation and Functionalism in Sociology* (London, Routledge and Kegan Paul, 1968), pp. 59–61. See also P. A. Weiss, 'The Living System: Determinism Stratified' in A. Koestler and J. R. Smythies (eds), *Beyond Reductionism* (London, Hutchinson, 1969), pp. 3–42, and, in the same collection, L. von Bertalanffy, 'Chance or Law' (pp. 63–76).

But supposing this argument is mistaken, and that teleological explanation is valid in biology; would this confer any validity on functional explanation in social science? Of the two forms of sociological functionalism, it appears that teleological explanation of the kind we have been discussing is more likely to be applicable to the institutional relation form. Any social parallel of biological homeostasis would seem to imply that some particular feature of a society remains constant; and where there is a functional relation between coexisting institutions, one tends to maintain the other in its existing form. At first sight, the analogy seems quite close.

However, it is not close enough. Teleological explanation of the relevant sort depends on teleological *laws*, stating that some feature of the system tends to *remain as it is* – not merely that a certain item tends to maintain that feature as it is. The former is a much more stringent requirement than the latter. It is perfectly possible that certain social forces tend to keep some feature of a social system as it is, but there is no general tendency for that feature to remain as it is, because there are equally strong (or stronger) forces making for change. This is, indeed, the situation of social systems. Societies are subject to both conservative and innovatory forces; they do not, generally speaking, possess negative feedback mechanisms strong enough to permit the assertion of teleological laws comparable with that which describes the tendency of the human body to remain constant at 37°C. This is not to deny that some negative feedback mechanisms are at work in social systems; the point is that there is no reason to think that, in general, they are more powerful than the forces making for structural change.

Even in cases where quasi-homeostatic social mechanisms do exist, functional/teleological explanations do not seem appropriate. Perhaps the best social analogue of biological homeostasis is the gold standard system as it operated before 1914. The system operated in such a way that a nation's external payments tended to keep just in balance. If its payments outwards exceeded the payments received, the resulting loss of gold caused a contraction of domestic credit which tended to decrease its outward payments (and perhaps increase its receipts); if receipts exceeded outward payments, the resulting inflow of gold had the opposite effect. Any deviation from balance thus tended to be self-cancelling. But it would seem ridiculous to explain the flows of gold which brought this about by their 'function' of maintaining the balance; they were the consequence of individuals settling international transactions. Of course, in so far as statesmen and others *wished* to achieve a balance of international payments, and maintained the gold standard system for that purpose, these facts enter into the explanation of its existence. But this is to explain the existence of the institution by their motives, not by its function. Thus, when it was decided, between the

I

two world wars, that the costs of the system (in unemployment, etc.) were too high, it ceased to exist.

What about the relevance of teleological explanation to societal survival functionalism? Could it not be argued that survival as a social system could count as a 'goal-state' of a society maintained by various forces within the society? Certainly it is a very unspecific goal-state, but that is perhaps not a decisive objection. Once again, however, the applicability of teleological explanation requires a suitable teleological law, which in this case would be 'Societies tend to survive' (in some form or other, that is). It is perhaps dubious whether this is true. Not only have some past societies perished completely; modern weapon technology, combined with the psychological propensities of the human race, suggests that the destruction of societies (perhaps all societies) is a distinct possibility in the future. But even if the law is true, it must be remembered that teleological explanation is in any case invalid. It would be very strange to say, for example, that modern health services, which promote societal survival, exist *because* they promote societal survival (though people's *awareness* of this might be part of the explanation). We must conclude that so-called teleological explanation adds nothing to the explanatory force of functional statements in social science.

CHAPTER 6

Value-judgements and Social Science

IN this final chapter we shall be concerned with the relation to the social sciences of 'value-judgements' (or 'evaluations'). Many controversial issues arise here; but, as often happens, distinctions are obscured by attaching different meanings to a single, very abstract term—in this case, 'value-free social science'—which thereby becomes almost meaningless. The concept was originally given currency by Max Weber, who is still widely taken as the classical exponent of 'value-freedom' (or *Wertfreiheit*), though what he meant by the expression is not always appreciated.

Weber maintains two positions, one a matter of metaphysics and logic, one a practical prescription. First, there exist two distinct and separate spheres, the sphere of facts and the sphere of values.[1] Correspondingly, there is a logical disjunction between statements of fact and statements expressing evaluations. Only the sphere of facts is the subject-matter of science, whether physical or social, for only facts, and not values, are ascertainable by the observational methods of science; science consists of statements of fact, not statements of value. Problems relating to the sphere of facts include: what phenomena exist in the world? what law-like relations hold between them? what explains them? By contrast, value-judgements are judgements of 'the satisfactory or unsatisfactory character of phenomena', of their 'desirability or undesirability'.[2] The sphere of values includes all problems as to what should be done in a given situation, and what states of affairs one should try to bring about – problems of rightness and goodness.

Weber's prescription is that the logical disjunction of facts and values should not be concealed or blurred.[3] Anyone who expresses a value-

---

[1] M. Weber, *The Methodology of the Social Sciences*, pp. 2, 11, 13, 18–25, 58–9, and *passim*.
[2] *Ibid.*, pp. 1, 10.   [3] *Ibid.*, pp. 2, 4, 60.

judgement should not pretend that it is scientifically warranted, since it cannot be. If social scientists make recommendations for action, they should be at pains to make clear that every such recommendation implies some extra-scientific evaluation, whatever scientifically established facts it also rests on – for laymen may not appreciate this. As Weber notes, his precept itself depends on a value-judgement: given the logical disjunction of fact and value, it follows from the principle of intellectual honesty. This value-principle is of course rarely attacked explicitly; Weber's critics, therefore, usually aim at the logical leg of his argument.

Why, one may wonder, was it necessary for Weber to make these points specifically in relation to *social* science? Logically, they apply to physical science equally. But the difference in subject-matter between the two kinds of science makes an important psychological difference. Human action is peculiarly the subject-matter of one particular, even pre-eminent, kind of value-judgement, the *moral* judgement. When moral judgements are applied to social facts, we enter the realm of politics, with its attendant passions and partisanship. These value-judgements, therefore, often generate powerful emotional pressures, which may influence judgements of fact, and lead to the blurring or denial of the fact-value distinction. Physical nature too may be the subject of value-judgements, but not of moral judgements – of praise, blame, or justification. We do not blame floods and earthquakes for killing men; we do blame individuals and governments for doing so – and often passionately. It is the passionate human desire to praise and blame that gives Weber's remarks their point. In effect, he asserts that, despite the *psychological* differences, the *logical* relation between social science and value-judgements about social facts is, in the respects indicated (not, in Weber's view, in all respects)[4] the same as that between physical science and value-judgements about physical nature.

Weber was extremely careful to spell out what this does, and especially does not, imply. For example, it does *not* imply that the sphere of values, least of all moral judgements, is unimportant: 'An *attitude of moral indifference* has no connection with *scientific* "objectivity".'[5] On the contrary – recognition of the fact-value disjunction is a necessary condition of meaningful moral argument. Again, Weber was well aware that all human *action* implies some value-judgement (the agent must hold that what he does is, for some reason, the right thing to do in the circumstances). Scientific activity is no exception; the practice of social science, the investigation of any subject therein, presupposes that the result sought is worth achieving.[6] Weber's point, simply, is that this result is knowledge of facts, not values. From the premise that

[4] Cf. below, pp. 147–50.
[5] *The Methodology of the Social Sciences*, p. 60.   [6] *Ibid.*, pp. 10–11.

factual knowledge is valuable, nothing whatever follows as to which facts are *true*. It does follow, naturally, that scientific procedures, experiments, etc., should be well adapted to discovering facts. *Methodological* value-judgements – evaluations of procedures and inferences, rules for the assessment of evidence, etc. – are part of the *technique* of science. But value-statements are no part of its *product*. Social science, of course, is not only itself a human activity, its subject-matter too is human activity, and it therefore seeks knowledge of the values of the people studied.[7] (Previous chapters should have made clear how aware Weber was of this.)[8] It does not follow that the social scientist himself holds or should hold the same or any other values. Despite all this, arguments against value-free social science frequently include objections to the positions from which Weber expressly dissociated himself.[9]

If, as Weber asserts, the rightness or wrongness of (non-methodological) value-judgements is irrelevant to the truth or falsity of statements of fact, one's factual assertions should not be influenced by irrelevant value-premises. Gunnar Myrdal pointed out, in *An American Dilemma*, one common way in which this happens, namely, a factual judgement is distorted by unwillingness to admit to conflict between *different* value-judgements.[10] Myrdal reported that many white Americans both accepted the principle of equality of opportunity, and believed that Negroes ought to be worse off than Whites – two value-judgements which conflict unless Negroes are inferior in ability. This, accordingly, the whites tended to assert, sometimes backing the assertion with a selective version of the relevant evidence. Conversely, someone who believed in equality of opportunity and also favoured equal treatment of the two races might 'deduce' from his two value-premises the factual assertion that Negroes and Whites are equal in ability. Similarly conflicting factual assertions occur frequently in the social sciences. For example, if a sociologist of education believes both that children of different levels of measured ability should, for social reasons, be educated together, and also that schools should be educationally effective, these two value-judgements may generate the factual assertion that children taught in 'comprehensive' schools have educational attainments equal to or better than those of children taught in segregated schools; while a second sociologist of education, who also values educational effectiveness but whose social attitudes lead him to favour

---

[7] *The Methodology of the Social Sciences*, pp. 11, 13.
[8] Cf. pp. 38–40 above.
[9] See, for example, A. R. Louch, *Explanation and Human Action* (Oxford, Blackwell, 1966), pp. 182, 184–5 (on value-neutral political science); L. Strauss *Natural Right and History* (Chicago U.P., 1953), p. 55; P. Streeten, Introduction to G. Myrdal, *Value in Social Theory*, p. xviii–xix.
[10] *An American Dilemma* (New York, Harper and Row, 1944), pp. 89, 97–108, 1027–31.

separate education of children of different ability, is liable to conclude that children taught in segregated schools have superior educational attainments. This factual disagreement does indeed exist.[11] Neither of the opposed conclusions is unsupported by (some) evidence, but clearly both cannot be based on the evidence alone. To allow value-premises to influence factual assertions in this way is, Weber argues, illegitimate – at best a form of self-deception, at worst of dishonesty.

His argument also implies the exclusion from social science of all *concepts* which are wholly or partly evaluative – for example 'justice'. What conditions make for a just society is a question outside the scope of social science, because 'a just society' means a society that is *good* in a major respect. This does not prevent anyone from spelling out his own conception of social justice in value-free terms (possibly as some specific distribution of wealth, opportunity, etc.), and investigating sociologically what conditions favour such a society. But to anyone having a different conception of social justice, these would not be conditions favouring a *just* society. A sociology of justice-as-such is, on Weber's view, impossible.

The distinction between evaluative and factual concepts can quite often be blurred, so as to lend a spuriously 'scientific' air to favoured value-judgements. Weber himself gives the example of 'adaptation', a term borrowed by several social sciences from biology.[12] The better 'adapted' an organism is to its environment, the more likely it is to reproduce. As applied to societies the term is vague, yet carries over-tones both evaluatively favourable and apparently 'scientific'. But as Weber points out, a society that is well adapted in the biological sense (i.e. rapidly increases its numbers) is not necessarily admirable. Because of the confusion of fact and value implicit in the term, it should be dropped. Similarly suspect is the term 'progress' which, says Weber,[13] is admissible in the social sciences only in the sense of technical progress, of increasing capacity to achieve given ends, which is a matter of fact. To rate change as 'progress' in an unqualified sense is a matter of value-judgements, not of science.

Weber's critique could be extended to many other terms current in social science. Marxist theory, for example, systematically uses terms

---

[11] See, for example, the contradictory conclusions of, on the one hand, Robin Pedley, *The Comprehensive School* (London, Penguin, 1966), pp. 96–8, repeated in the revised edn (Penguin, 1969), pp. 105–9; on the other, R. Davis, *The Grammar School* (London, Penguin, 1967), pp. 133–7, and contributors to the *Black Paper* series (edited by C. B. Cox and A. E. Dyson, London, Critical Quarterly Society) such as A. Pollard and R. R. Pedley (*Black Paper Two*, pp. 75–6 and p. 83 respectively) and J. Todd (*Black Paper Three*, pp. 48–53). I am grateful to Mrs Doreen McBarnet for providing most of these references.

[12] *The Methodology of the Social Sciences*, pp. 25–6.

[13] *Ibid.*, pp. 27–36.

that blend factual and evaluative meanings. Capitalism, according to Marxist theory, is riddled with 'contradictions' which will eventually bring about its downfall. According to Engels, the 'fundamental contradiction' from which all the others stem is the 'contradiction between socialized production and capitalistic appropriation'.[14] That is; production is a co-operative process to which many men, mostly wage-earners, contribute, but the fruits of their labour are largely appropriated by a few individuals, the capitalists; this is a 'contradiction'. Clearly Engels does not mean that it is a *logical* contradiction. Rather he seems to mean two things: first, that this state of affairs is *unjust* (a value-judgement); second, that it leads to *conflict* between wage-earners and capitalists, and also to inefficiency ('anarchy') which intensifies the conflict (judgements of fact). There is no objection whatever, on Weberian principles, to making both sorts of assertion, but to embrace both in the single term 'contradiction' obscures the fact that two different sorts of statement are being made.

Another popular sociological term that often offends against Weber's precepts is 'function'. In the usages discussed in chapter 5,[15] this means a contribution to maintaining a social system either in its existing form ('institutional relation functionalism') or in any form whatever ('societal survival functionalism') – both factual meanings. But in addition the expression can be understood evaluatively, to mean either a *desirable* effect of some social practice, or the effect it *ought* to produce (its task, so to speak). So many possible meanings provide plentiful opportunities for blurring the fact-value distinction. Even confusing the two factual meanings can suggest unwarranted evaluative conclusions, for if anything is functional in the societal survival sense that for most people would be an argument in its favour, while the same is not necessarily true of a function in the institutional relation sense. Examples of this confusion were given in chapter 5. (The corresponding ambiguity of 'dysfunction', we saw, not infrequently leads to a confusion between *change* and *disorder*).[16] Attribution even of a societal survival function to a practice may reflect a favourable value-judgement rather than convincing evidence, which is often hard to come by; attribution simply of a 'function' is often no more than an attempt to invest such a value-judgement with the authority of 'science'.

An example of the ambiguities to which the term 'function' is prone is provided by a well-known political theory put forward by Gabriel Almond[17] and applied by his collaborators. According to Almond,

[14] F. Engels, *Socialism Utopian and Scientific*, reprinted in *The Essential Left* (London, Allen and Unwin, 1960), pp. 145, 129–41.

[15] See pp. 112–3 above.   [16] See above, pp. 114–7.

[17] G. A. Almond and J. S. Coleman (eds), *The Politics of the Developing Areas* (Princeton U.P. paperback, 1970), pp. 7, 12–17, 33–45.

every society has a *political system*, which helps to perform 'the functions of integration and adaptation'. By 'integration' Almond apparently means the maintenance of order (a societal survival function); what he means by 'adaptation' is not at all clear (Weber's remarks are entirely apposite here) beyond the fact that it refers to change of some sort. But he holds that the performance of these functions involves the carrying on of certain processes, which he calls 'political functions'. Two of these are of interest here: the 'articulation of interests' and the 'aggregation of interests' (that is, respectively, making demands for the furthering of interests of members of the society, and framing a policy which combines and compromises these demands). Yet it appears that in some functioning political systems these processes are more or less absent. Lucian Pye, applying Almond's functional framework to political systems in South-East Asia, reports that the 'potential interests' of the mass of people are not effectively articulated (the qualification 'potential' here seems meaningless or inaccurate) and political leaders to a large extent 'seek to act as representatives of all their peoples and not as brokers aggregating specific interests'.[18] What, then, does Almond mean by picking out interest articulation and aggregation as 'political functions'? That these processes are necessary to social order and/or change? This is implausible. The likeliest answer is that Almond thinks of these processes as a *desirable* way of maintaining order in society, and of bringing about change (probably Almond's 'function' of 'adaptation' simply boils down to desirable change). There is little doubt that for Pye their absence was a moral fault in South-East Asian political systems. (It is after all part of the democratic faith that policy should reflect the felt needs of ordinary people.) In other words, Almond's functional model is to a large degree evaluative, but not explicitly so.

The nature of moral judgements

We turn now to criticisms of Weber's disjunction of facts and values, and in particular of facts and moral values. Views as to the nature of moral judgements are commonly divided into two kinds, 'subjectivist' and 'objectivist'. On the subjectivist view, a person's moral evaluation of any phenomenon *expresses his attitude* (favourable or unfavourable) to it; on the objectivist view, it *describes* the phenomenon, attributing to it (correctly or incorrectly) a moral characteristic which it objectively possesses or lacks. The subjectivist view poses no problem for Weber's programme, which becomes an injunction to distinguish clearly between facts, and the social scientist's attitudes towards them. But on the objectivist view, moral qualities are actually a kind of fact. There are broadly two objectivist views as to what kind of facts they are. Some

[18] G. A. Almond and J. S. Coleman (eds), *The Politics of the Developing Areas*, pp. 119, 124.

thinkers hold that they are equivalent to *natural* (i.e. non-moral) facts; that, for example, 'x is good' is a true statement if and only if x is conducive to human happiness, or accords with the trend of evolution, or whatever. The other objectivist view is that moral qualities are facts *sui generis*, capable of being apprehended by correct use of the appropriate intellectual faculty (intuition, moral sense, reason, etc.), but not reducible to natural facts.[19]

Weber himself took a subjectivist view of moral judgement: individuals' 'ultimate evaluations' are something they have to choose, and their choices may be 'unbridgeably divergent'; 'to *judge* the *validity* of such values is a matter of *faith*', not of reason.[20] To Leo Strauss, one of Weber's most trenchant critics, this ethical theory is the fundamental error lying behind his call for value-free social science.[21] For Strauss moral truth is an objective fact. We *know*, for example, that cruelty and tyranny are evil, and we *know* what sorts of behaviour are cruel and tyrannical – we can recognize them when we see them. Far from its being unscientific to describe behaviour in these terms, to avoid them is unscientific – it is failing to 'understand social phenomena as what they are'. That is, the most important thing about, say, Nazi concentration camps is that they were a cruel and evil phenomenon. Given that we know good from evil, this knowledge should direct all social science: social scientists should (presumably) devote themselves to discovering how to abolish cruelty and tyranny, how to achieve social justice, etc.

If Strauss were right about the nature of morality, the kind of social science he advocates would be possible, but not the only one possible. Moral terms (such as cruelty, tyranny, justice) would be scientifically acceptable descriptions of social phenomena; but so would value-free terms (such as imprisonment, monarchy, stratification). There is no warrant for Strauss's claim that only the moral concepts capture what social phenomena 'are', and provide the only basis for understanding them; for undoubtedly value-free descriptions can also be correctly applied to them. No doubt a morally oriented social science, if possible, is itself a moral imperative, but there is no reason why a more theoretical interest in social life should be considered illegitimate. From the point of view, say, of framing social theories of as general application as possible, the value-free concepts might be more useful than moral ones, even if Strauss is right about moral truth.

Nevertheless, it is true that explanations of social phenomena and generalizations about them are quite often framed in moral terms. It

---

[19] Cf. the similar trichotomy in Q. Gibson, *op. cit.*, pp. 60–3.
[20] *The Methodology of the Social Sciences*, pp. 14, 55.
[21] *Natural Right and History*, pp. 36, 40–53; *What is Political Philosophy?* (New York, Free Press, 1959), p. 95.

would be quite normal to explain, say, the French Revolution by the *injustice* of the social structure under the Ancien Régime, and even to assert the generalization that '*oppression* (i.e. severe injustice) always leads to rebellion'. Causal attribution of this kind is, we saw, implicit in Engels' use of the term 'contradictions'.[22] Other writers have suggested that the explanation of action may require reference to the moral qualities of the action and the agent. Quentin Gibson, for example, suggests that perhaps this is how one should explain why men throughout history have striven for liberty – that is, the explanation may be that liberty is good, and some men at least desire the good.[23] Recently, too, John Rawls has put forward, as part of a theory of justice, three 'laws of moral psychology' according to which the justice of institutions influences the attitudes of individuals; thus, one of his laws asserts that if a person who through an appropriate upbringing has acquired certain normal psychological capacities is associated with others in a social arrangement which is both just and known to be just, he will develop feelings of friendship and trust towards those of his associates who do what the rules of the arrangement require of them.[24]

The question raised by these various laws and explanations is not whether they are true, but whether, framed as they are, they could form part of an objective social science. It seems clear that they cannot. Suppose first of all that the moral qualities of situations (goodness, justness, etc.) are objective facts *sui generis*, not corresponding to 'natural' facts. The obvious difficulty is how to recognize them; for it remains true that different people judge differently whether they are present or absent in a given case. If we know that cruelty is wrong, this is to know only a tautology; to call behaviour 'cruel' already implies that it is wrong. When it comes to designating particular behaviour as cruel, or particular social arrangements as just, there is (despite Strauss) no general agreement. This may be because some people have an accurate and others a defective moral sense or intuition, but the problem is to know, and demonstrate, which is which. This problem has never been solved. Thus, *even if the subjectivist view of morality is mistaken, from the standpoint of social science it might as well be right.* Even if it is true that oppression always leads to rebellion (and so on), such a proposition cannot be scientifically tested. It cannot be shown that anything is evidence for or against it.

Fortunately these propositions lend themselves to reformulation in a value-free way, in terms of moral beliefs instead of moral qualities: men pursue liberty because (rightly or wrongly) they *believe* it to be good, rather than because it *is* good; not injustice and oppression but what men believe (rightly or wrongly) to be unjust and oppressive

[22] See above, p. 135. [23] *Op. cit.*, p. 64.
[24] J. Rawls, *A Theory of Justice* (Cambridge, Harvard U.P., 1971), p. 490.

moves them to rebellion. As for Rawls' laws of moral psychology, their meaning is more equivocal than at first appears. In later discussion, while insisting that 'some conception of justice' must play a part in moral learning, Rawl admits that it may 'belong solely to the psychological theory and not [be] . . . accepted as philosophically correct'.[25] This perhaps means that what is involved is not after all the justice of social arrangements but whether people believe them to be just.

Suppose, now, that moral qualities are objective and correspond to 'natural' facts. In that case, as Gibson has noted, moral and value-free descriptions would be interchangeable and it would not matter which were used in social science.[26] The great difficulty, however, is to know *which* natural qualities are the equivalent of moral ones. Unfortunately there is no general agreement on this. There are, for example, many different 'conceptions' of justice, as Rawl calls them. To 'classical' utilitarians, justice (like all good) is maximum possible happiness; he himself has argued for a conception which makes it, in summary, 'a complex of three ideas: liberty, equality and reward for services [to the community]'· Clearly, unless one particular naturalist view can be shown to be right, naturalism avoids none of the difficulties of the *sui generis* brand of moral objectivism. Let us therefore consider some popular naturalist theories.

A prominent critic of the fact-value dichotomy in relation to social science who has recently argued for a quasi-utilitarian naturalism is Charles Taylor.[27] He claims that anything which conduces to human happiness, or to the fulfilment of human wants and purposes, is to that extent good (though it may have bad features too). For Taylor that is not a value-judgement, but an account of the *logic* of the concept of goodness. But is it self-contradictory to deny that goodness has anything to do with human happiness? It would seem not. It is not illogical, for example, to hold that freedom is good, even the greatest good, regardless of whether men want it and of whether it makes them happy, on the ground that it is their *duty* to make their own decisions and assume responsibility for their own lives, burdensome though that might be. (Both Marx and John Stuart Mill can indeed be interpreted as holding this position.) Again, there need be nothing logically inconsistent in a religious ethic according to which goodness depends not at all on human happiness or purposes but entirely on conformity to God's will, which might in principle (some theologians have believed) be anything at all.

[25] J. Rawls, *A Theory of Justice*, p. 496.
[26] Q. Gibson, *op. cit.*, p. 62.
[27] C. Taylor, 'Neutrality in Political Science', in P. Laslett and W. G. Runciman (eds), *Philosophy, Politics, and Society, third series* (Oxford, Blackwell, 1967), pp. 48–55.

Even if we were to accept that human happiness and the satisfaction of human wants are always good, and nothing else is except what conduces to them, this would not permit the reduction of moral qualities to natural facts, because it tells us nothing about the right *distribution* of happiness and satisfaction among different individuals. It tells us nothing, that is, about *justice*. In a situation of scarcity, where different individuals are in competition for satisfactions, no action or situation can be rated as right or good without an evaluation of its distributive implications. Quasi-utilitarian naturalist ethics as exemplified by Taylor is of no help in choosing between different conceptions of justice, and thus fails to make justice, rightness, or goodness a scientifically usable concept.

This emerges very clearly from the chequered history of 'welfare economics', a would-be social science posited on utilitarian ethical assumptions.[28] The 'economic welfare' of a community was equated with the net satisfactions that accrue to its members from their economic activities; it was also treated as an evaluative concept in the sense that more welfare is better than less. Welfare economists wanted, by studying the conditions that would increase a community's welfare, to make *scientific prescriptions*. They soon ran into trouble. If a given change would increase everyone's satisfaction, or decrease everyone's satisfaction, there is no problem; but if (as is usually the case) it would increase some people's satisfactions at the expense of others, the question of distribution – of justice – immediately arises. Welfare economists came to realize they could say nothing both scientific and prescriptive about such cases. By and large they now confine the expression 'increase in economic welfare' to a change that makes no-one worse off, and makes some people (or even a single person) better off. If such a change is possible, the situation is described as non-optimal; if not, it is a *Pareto optimum*. But there is no unique Pareto optimum for any given set of resources – there are indefinitely many, each with a different distribution of satisfactions, between which economic science cannot choose.

In sum, even granted the disputable assumptions of a Taylorian ethics, the scientific usefulness of an evaluative concept of economic welfare is very limited. At one point, Nicholas Kaldor[29] attempted to escape from these limitations by proposing a broader criterion of increased welfare: any change increases economic welfare if it would make it *possible* to make everyone better off than before (that is, any

[28] Cf. I. M. D. Little, *A Critique of Welfare Economics* (London, Oxford U.P., 1950), pp. 76–82, 86; E. J. Mishan, 'A Survey of Welfare Economics, 1939–59', *Economic Journal*, vol. 70 (1960), p. 199.

[29] 'Welfare Propositions of Economics and Inter-Personal Comparisons of Utility', *Economic Journal*, vol. 49 (1939), pp. 549–52.

losers could be more than compensated out of the gains of others by some redistributive mechanism). Questions of *the right distribution* of satisfactions, Kaldor argued, are in a different category – that of politics, not science. But Kaldor was certainly wrong to suppose that his criterion can be the basis of 'scientific prescriptions'.[30] Whether a change that conforms to it should be made still depends partly on considerations of justice. Gunnar Myrdal has claimed that the inevitably evaluative nature of the concept of economic welfare illustrates the general futility of trying to avoid value-loaded terms in social science.[31] The contrary is the case. What the saga of welfare economics demonstrates is the impossibility of a prescriptive science based on evaluative concepts.

Let us turn now to another popular brand of ethical naturalism, the *evolutionary*. One variety of this may be called Hegelian-Marxist, and is exemplified in the writings of Herbert Marcuse.[32] Marcuse attacks the fact-value dichotomy by distinguishing how things *appear* from their *essence* or true nature, which is also what they *ought* to be. Essences, especially the essence of *man*, are revealed in history: 'given facts . . . are appearances whose essence can be comprehended only in the context of particular historical tendencies aiming at a different form of reality'. The political implication of Marcuse's doctrine can be expressed in the words of Durkheim (also, apparently, subject to Hegelian influences): 'The society that morality bids us desire is not the society as it appears to itself, but the society as it really is or is becoming'.[33] From this it follows that any successful attempt to change society – in whatever way – must be morally justified, while failure in such an attempt is a sign of moral error if not depravity; success or failure is the verdict of history, the revealer of essences, of what should be. There is no reason whatever to accept such a view.[34]

Another variety of evolutionary ethics may be dubbed the *biological*, two modern exponents of which are the geneticist C. H. Waddington and the psychologist B. F. Skinner.[35] Both these writers believe that biological evolution has an identifiable direction, and that this indi-

---

[30] Cf. I. M. D. Little, *op. cit.*, pp. 89–94.

[31] G. Myrdal, *Objectivity in Social Research* (London, Duckworth, 1970), p. 57.

[32] See his *Negations* (London, Allen Lane, 1968), pp. 69 ff.

[33] E. Durkheim, *Sociology and Philosophy*, reprinted in G. Simpson (ed.), *Emile Durkheim* (New York, Crowell, 1963), p. 115. For a possible link between Durkheim and Hegelianism, see F. A. Hayek, *op. cit.*, pp. 204–5.

[34] Nor has Marcuse always done so. As Alasdair MacIntyre points out (*Marcuse*, Fontana, 1970, p. 62) he has had periods of moral pessimism about the future.

[35] See Waddington, *The Ethical Animal* (London, Allen and Unwin, 1960), esp. pp. 59, 78, 134–7, 148–51; Skinner, *op. cit.*, pp. 102–3, 136, 138–43, 172–4.

cates the direction in which *social* evolution *ought* to proceed. For Waddington, the trend of organic evolution is towards organisms with increasing independence of, and control over, their environment; human practices, therefore, are good to the extent that they further these ends. Skinner, for his part, picks out as the crucial evolutionary trend an increasing sensitivity of behaviour to its consequences, that is, the consequences of various types of behaviour increasingly control how the organism behaves. For Skinner, the evolutionary significance of 'culture' is that it allows human behaviour to be brought under the control of remote consequences; hence, whatever social practices bring remote consequences of action into play are good.

Why should one suppose that the direction of evolution provides the criterion of goodness? For Skinner (and probably, though less explicitly, for Waddington too), it is because the more evolved an organism is in this direction, the better are its chances of survival. Skinner holds, in other words, that morality can be reduced to survival value. But even granting that the survival of the human species is a good thing, it would be absurd to suppose that it is ultimately the only good thing, so that the whole of morality can be derived from this principle. More fundamentally, the facts of evolution may allow us to infer what features make for survival; they cannot show that survival is good, much less the only or supreme good.

We must conclude that neither utilitarian nor evolutionary naturalism can provide an adequate account of morality. Without investigating all actual or possible naturalistic ethics, it seems safe to conclude that none of them can be proved. Thus, even if some brand of naturalism is correct, the heterogeneity of moral judgements remains, rendering moral concepts scientifically useless.

Moral objections to value-free social science

Let us now tackle the question from a different direction. Instead of looking for a logical basis for an evaluative social science, we shall discuss arguments alleging that value-free social science is in some way objectionable.

One not infrequent charge is that Weber's position leads to *moral nihilism*. Weber himself was certainly no nihilist: he held that in the individual's choice of his own values lies 'the dignity of the "person-ality" ',[36] But if moral values have only a subjective validity, object-ively speaking the moral universe consists only of innumerable con-flicting values between which no rational choice is possible. Weber's thesis, charges Strauss, implies the equality of all values; a value-free social science, therefore, 'is born to be the handmaid of any powers or

[36] M. Weber, *The Methodology of the Social Sciences*, p. 55.

interests that be, . . . to give advice with equal competence and alacrity to tyrants as well as to free peoples'.[37] Again, Alasdair MacIntyre asserts that the exclusion of moral concepts from social science implies that moral qualities cannot be causally effective in social life, hence that justice, for example, 'can play no part' in politics – and since this nihilistic implication is really 'the most extreme of value-commitments', the principle of value-freedom is actually self-contradictory.[38]

But whether or not moral nihilism is the logical conclusion of the subjectivist theory of ethics (a question that need not be discussed here), it is not implied by the doctrine of value-free social science. That doctrine does not exclude the possibility that certain moral principles and judgements are right; it presupposes, rather, that their rightness cannot be rationally demonstrated (perhaps owing to some defect of the human intellect), and hence moral concepts are unsuited to the scientific method. This being so, the value-freedom doctrine cannot lend support to *any* particular moral position; it no more implies such nihilistic positions as that politicians need not worry about justice, or that social scientists need not scruple to advise evil men on how to further their evil ends, than it implies the contrary positions. It is true, of course, that a neutral social science can be misused by evil men; but so, equally, could a Straussian social science, if one were possible. Knowledge of the conditions that promote social justice and injustice, for example, could be used to frustrate the former and defend the latter, if any 'powers' so wished. It is an inescapable fact that knowledge can always be misused.

But if the value-freedom doctrine does not imply moral nihilism in relation to the ends that social science is used to promote, it does so, according to some critics, in relation to the *means* used to promote them. The doctrine implies, they hold, that the choice of ends is a matter of values, and hence cannot be prescribed by science; but that, given the end to be pursued, the question of whether and how it can be achieved is a matter of fact; hence it falls within the province of the social scientist (acting, perhaps, as expert adviser to a government) to prescribe the means for achieving given social ends. Gunnar Myrdal has pointed out,[39] however, that it is an error to suppose, even given the desirability of the end, that no further evaluative questions arise in prescribing the means. Any measure that may be prescribed as a means is properly subject to evaluation *in itself*; and any such measure may have *other* consequences, desirable or undesirable, besides the given end. An example may make this clearer. Suppose that the government

[37] L. Strauss, *Natural Right and History*, pp. 4–5, 41–2.
[38] A. MacIntyre, *Against the Self-Images of the Age* (London, Duckworth, 1971), pp. 277–8.
[39] See his *Value in Social Theory*, pp. 49–50.

of a poor country asks an economist how it can promote economic growth, and that one possible way is to reduce the population's consumption so that investment can increase. Now, to lower the living standards of poor people is *in itself* a measure subject to (possibly negative) evaluation; it may, besides, lead to so much discontent that order can be maintained only by repression. Before prescribing any measure as a means to economic development or anything else, Myrdal says, the social scientist must evaluate the desirability of alternative means in themselves, and of their possible or probable further consequences; and this, allegedly, is denied by the value-freedom doctrine. According to A. R. Louch,[40] that doctrine leads the social scientist as adviser to draw only on his knowledge of value-free factual relationships, and hence to prescribe the *most efficient* means to the desired end, regardless of its moral (or aesthetic) implications. Such an attitude he dubs 'totalitarian' (meaning that it implies total commitment to a single end regardless of other considerations).

Myrdal's contention that policy recommendations neither can nor should be value-free is certainly correct; but this does not imply that social science should not be value-free. To prescribe a means (whether the most efficient or some other) to a given end, like any prescription, goes beyond science. Science can warrant only statements of the expected consequences of various possible measures; in principle, an 'expert adviser' can, if he chooses, limit himself to giving his employer information of this kind. If he chooses to *recommend* some specific course of action, it should be clearly understood that his recommendation cannot be warranted by scientific knowledge. Weber himself pointed out very clearly precisely this distinction, and relation, between science and policy;[41] Myrdal is thus absolutely wrong to accuse him of advocating value-free, 'scientific', policy recommendations.[42]

Another common charge against value-free social science is that, indirectly, it actually upholds a particular value-position or social interest – usually, the *status quo*.[43] A view popular among Marxists and 'critical' social scientists is that Weber's doctrine is really a conservative 'ideology', which discredits criticism of the *status quo* by denying that it can be scientific. This charge has no justification. If it is true that the

[40] *Op. cit.*, p. 190.   [41] *The Methodology of the Social Sciences*, pp. 18–19, 20–1, 37–8, 53.   [42] See G. Myrdal, *Value in Social Theory*, pp. 208–9.
[43] See, for example, A. W. Gouldner, 'Anti-Minotaur: The Myth of a Value-Free Sociology' in I. L. Horowitz (ed.), *The New Sociology* (New York, Oxford U.P., 1964), pp. 205–7, as well as the editor's Introduction, pp. 9–10; also M. Nicolaus, 'The Professional Organization of Sociology' in R. Blackburn (ed.), *Ideology in Social Science* (London, Fontana, 1972), p. 49; H. Zinn, 'History as Private Enterprise', quoted in G. Nettler, *Explanations* (New York, McGraw-Hill, 1970), p. 180; and the discussion of Horkheimer in M. Jay, *The Dialectical Imagination* (London, Heinemann, 1973), p. 80.

denial of scientific status to value-judgements lessens the self-confidence of critics of the established order, this is simply a psychological fact – it does not imply that the denial is mistaken. Probably, too, it is a psychological fact resulting from a logical error, namely, the belief that if science cannot criticize the *status quo* it must justify it. A value-free social science, of course, can do no such thing – it gives no support to any particular value-position. Many upholders of the fact-value disjunction have in fact been radicals[44] (and Weber himself attacked as hypocritical 'the pseudo-"ethically neutral" prophet who speaks for the dominant interests').[45]

A variation on this theme is provided by Paul Streeten,[46] who alleges that the value-freedom doctrine provides an ideological justification for laissez-faire liberalism (it is interesting to compare this with Louch's charge that it justifies totalitarianism). This argument is basically the same as Strauss's on nihilism; if no value-judgement is scientific, there is no basis for condemning any action, and hence no basis for preventing anyone doing whatever he pleases. Actually liberal philosophies usually advocate freedom only within limits, recognizing an area in which it must be curtailed. But support for freedom and opposition to it are equally value-judgements; a value-free social science lends no support to either.

So much for objections to value-free social science on moral grounds. We shall also, however, have to discuss a more radical class of objections, which allege that the doctrine prescribes something *logically impossible*. Since these arguments often involve an implicit or explicit contrast between the social and physical sciences, let us first consider the relation of value-judgements to the subject matter of the latter, and the question of their 'objectivity'.

Physical science, value-judgements, and objectivity
Value-free physical science is a relatively modern phenomenon, a product of the scientific and philosophical revolution of the sixteenth and seventeenth centuries. The conceptual framework of medieval science (Aristotelian in inspiration) was, as Alexandre Koyré has put it,[47] a cosmos 'in which the hierarchy of value determined the hierarchy and structure of being'. The world was conceived as a hierarchy of concentric spheres with the 'dark, heavy, and imperfect earth' occupying the most ignoble – central – position, and rising above it 'the higher

---

[44] Cf. A. MacIntyre, *Marcuse*, p. 19.
[45] *Methodology of the Social Sciences*, p. 9. See also pp. 6 and 10.
[46] In his Introduction to G. Myrdal, *Value in Social Theory*, p. xliii.
[47] See his *From the Closed World to the Infinite Universe* (Baltimore, Johns Hopkins Press paperback, 1968), pp. 2, 19–23, 29–30, 33. My own account is heavily dependent on Koyré's.

and higher perfection of the stars and heavenly spheres'. The fusion of facts and values involved is manifest in the arguments of thinkers steeped in this tradition. One of the first men to challenge the traditional view of the earth's position, Nicholas of Cusa, supported his heterodox opinion by arguing that the earth is *not* uniquely low and despicable – its 'noble and spherical' shape, its circular motion, the fact that it is larger than the moon and (viewed from an appropriate position) as brilliant in colour as the sun, all show this. Copernicus, by contrast, included among his arguments against the geocentric universe the postulate that the earth *is* baser than the brilliant sun. For Copernicus the central position is the noblest, and 'the condition of being at rest is . . . nobler and more divine than that of change and inconstancy'; hence the sun sits motionless at the centre of the universe, and the earth moves round it. Summarizing these arguments, for Copernicus the earth cannot be at the centre of the universe because it is less noble than the sun and stars; for Nicholas of Cusa it cannot be at the centre of the universe because it is no less noble than the sun and stars; for the orthodox medieval cosmology it must be at the centre of the universe because it is less noble than the sun and stars. It is obvious that arguments conducted in these terms cannot get anywhere.[48]

Argument in the physical sciences of today is of course very different, so much so that its conclusions can be said (despite the fashionable heterodoxy of T. S. Kuhn)[49] to represent the 'rational consensus'[50] of the moment. How is physical science able to achieve this objectivity? Popper[51] has pointed out that it is not because physical scientists are unprejudiced, objective-minded individuals – they can be passionately prejudiced in favour of particular theories (especially their own). But individual prejudice neither prevents consensus nor dictates it, because (says Popper) of two crucial characteristics of scientific *communities*. First, there is *freedom* to propose and criticize theories (this is necessary if the consensus is to be rational rather than dogmatic). But freedom by itself could bring a chaos of conflicting views – hence (second), scientists must (and do) accept a specific *discipline*: theories must be couched in *testable* form (cf. chapter 1). This allows controversies to be decided by 'public experience' (i.e. experience that everyone who takes the trouble can repeat), and willingness to accept this impersonal arbiter permits the rational concensus to emerge. So long as these scientific norms are

[48] It is not suggested that such arguments were the *only* ones used. But they carried weight.

[49] See his *The Structure of Scientific Revolutions* (Chicago U.P., 1962). In point of fact, it is not quite clear how important Kuhn takes the irrational elements in scientific beliefs to be, for different passages of his work display very different emphases—cf. for example, pp. 92–3, 150, 152–3, 156–7, 165–8.

[50] The phrase is borrowed from John Ziman, *op. cit.*, p. 9.

[51] *The Open Society and its Enemies*, vol. 2, pp. 216–18.

adequately operative in the communities of science, individual prejudice is so to speak smoothed out. They do not, of course, operate perfectly; but in the physical sciences they do so to an impressive degree.

In the social sciences the smoothing out process works much less well, partly (we saw) because of the greater intensity of passions generated by social issues – the extra-scientific value-commitments of social scientists may be stronger than their commitment to the norms of science. In addition social scientists face a genuine difficulty connected with Popper's principle of testability. Testability in physical science is not just a matter of couching hypotheses in a particular form; it also requires *methods* of testing them, notably the controlled experiment. Because of the notorious disadvantages under which social science labours in this respect, the implications of known facts for the truth-status of hypotheses are often very dubious. In this situation, the only rational course is to admit uncertainty, but there are many pressures for more definite conclusions (perhaps as a basis for action). Such conclusions are liable to be wishful thinking controlled by value-commitments rather than evidence.

These facts help to explain why Popperian scientific method works markedly less well in the social sciences: they in no way justify a value-laden social science. But Popper's analysis raises further questions.

Scientific concepts and value-relevance
Popper remarks that one valuable consequence of the practice of couching theories in testable form is that it enables scientists to speak a common language, and thus to avoid arguing at cross-purposes. It is possible to describe the world in a great many different ways, using alternative cross-cutting sets of concepts; the scientific method, as Popper describes it, forces scientists to seek the concepts best suited to framing the most general laws that can be corroborated by experience. It is in pursuit of this goal that physicists, for example, have come to conceptualize the world in terms of atoms, electrons, photons, etc. – these terms constitute their common language. In Popper's view, the troubles of the social sciences stem mainly from a failure to apply this aspect of scientific method; instead of framing hypotheses that can be tested (for example, in attempts to solve practical problems), they too often indulge in 'scholasticism' and 'verbal fireworks'.[52]

But there are many writers who disagree fundamentally with Popper's diagnosis and prescription, for reasons connected with the role of value-judgements. Among them is Weber himself. For Weber is the apostle not only of *value-freedom* (*Wertfreiheit*) in social science, but also of *value-relevance* (*Wertbeziehung*).[53] Weber holds that our interest in the

[52] *The Open Society and its Enemies*, vol. 2, pp. 221–2.
[53] *The Methodology of the Social Sciences*, 21–2, 72–82.

social world is of a different nature from that in the physical world; it is not an interest in subsuming particular phenomena under laws, but in phenomena which are *relevant to our values*. Furthermore, since different investigators have different values they are interested in different aspects of social phenomena, and hence conceptualize them differently. Physicists' language – atom, electron, etc. – reflects, not any evaluative interest in these phenomena, but a common desire to find the laws of nature; in social science, the multiplicity of points of view precludes any common language at all.

Weber's point here is rather clearly illustrated by an activity which bulks large in the social sciences, the construction of *typologies*. Consider for example the typologies used to classify political systems. Lucian Pye, in the work alluded to above, divided the *party systems* of South-East Asian States into two kinds: 'essentially one-party systems' and 'competitive party systems'.[54] In the first category he included North Vietnam (a dictatorial one-party régime) as well as Malaya and Burma (in which, at the time of writing, a single party had achieved a monopoly of government by defeating its rivals at the polls); in the second category Pye put both the Philippines (then ruled by a President chosen by popular vote from among party nominees and an elected legislature dominated by these parties), and Thailand (where government was exercized by agents of a hereditary monarch and most members of the assembly were nominees of the executive). Pye's typology presumably reflects what he takes to be the important distinctions among party systems; another observer, however, might hold that what matters is not whether a single party is numerically dominant, but whether the party system allows the people as a whole to choose their rulers – that is, whether parties can compete freely for executive and legislative power on the basis of free popular elections. On the basis of this value-judgement, the party systems of Malaya, Burma, and the Philippines (as they were in the 1950s) would be classed together as (more or less) 'democratic', those of North Vietnam and Thailand as 'autocratic'. Still another observer might prefer to classify party systems on the basis of whether they are controlled by a Marxist part – and so on. No one typology is right or wrong – any man's typology can seem perverse or irrelevant to another. And the same is true of all concepts, for all concepts are ways of classifying phenomena.

Weber was careful to point out that his doctrine of value-relevance does not imply that social science concepts must pick out phenomena that are *positively* valued by the social scientist – their importance to him may be as evils rather than as goods (cf. criminology, conflict

[54] G. A. Almond and J. S. Coleman (eds), *The Politics of the Developing Areas*, pp. 113–14.

theory, etc.). And this doctrine in no way conflicts with, or detracts from, the doctrine of value-freedom. While the investigator's values determine his concepts, and thus the subject-matter of his assertions, nevertheless these concepts must be *definable* in value-free terms, and *what* is asserted about this subject-matter must, to be scientific, exclude all value-judgements. In assessing the truth of these (factual) assertions, value-judgements (other than methodological) remain irrelevant. As Weber puts it, the statements of the social sciences are not 'subjective' in the sense of being valid for one person only, they simply interest different people to a different degree.[55]

Even so, Weber's doctrine of value-relevance seems somewhat to exaggerate the difference between social and physical science. As Talcott Parsons has remarked,[56] the effort to subsume particular facts under general laws is one possible focus of interest in the social world. (Weber's own conception of ideal typical theory seems to presuppose this.)[57] Conversely, we are also interested in the physical world from the point of view of relevance to our values, and our commonsense concepts reflect this (we talk of health and disease, deserts and fertile places, because of the profound relevance to our values of what these concepts pick out). Our practical interest in controlling physical phenomena (in promoting health and fertility, etc.) is closely linked to the theoretical scientific interest in general laws, which are a powerful instrument of control. But value-relevant concepts such as health and disease do not normally appear in the basic theoretical laws, which are highly general and abstract, and are relevant to practical control indirectly; particular cases of disease, for example, can be cured, and health restored, by applying knowledge of laws of biochemistry and physiology which refer to neither 'health' nor 'disease'.[58] In seeking to reduce all general knowledge to as few and as general basic theoretical propositions as possible, physical science renders the connection between its theoretical concepts and the value-relevant concepts of common sense increasingly indirect, at the same time as it renders practical control more effective.

In social science too, of course, general knowledge is (or would be) practically useful (in promoting, say, economic growth, or democratic or 'competitive' party systems). But most social sciences lack a framework of basic theoretical propositions from which generalizations at a lower level can be derived; in this situation, social scientists try to

---

[55] *The Methodology of the Social Sciences*, p. 84.
[56] *The Structure of Social Action* (New York, Free Press paperback, 1968), vol. II, pp. 595–8.
[57] See above, pp. 58–60.
[58] See above, p. 27. This indicates how phenomena can be scientifically explained by laws which do not refer to them directly.

generalize directly about the kinds of phenomena that seem important to them. This, perhaps, helps to explain why in the social sciences competing conceptual schemes proliferate, while in the physical sciences each community does use what Popper calls a common language. Another possible reason for the difference is that a good deal of the work of social scientists is descriptive in a fairly simple sense, without reference to laws or predictions; hence the concepts they use naturally reflect their interests.

Often, too, they are rather similar to concepts of everyday language, and this, together with their value-relevance, gives rise to some special problems.

Operationalization and indices

Everyday concepts are usually not very precise. To be used in scientific research (i.e. 'operationalized') they have to be made much more specific. Very often, though, the social scientist has to choose between alternative possibilities – a point much stressed by Gunnar Myrdal. Myrdal gives as an example the problem of tracing changes in the level of wages.[59] 'Level of wages' is a rather vague expression – it could refer either to average *annual* wage income per worker, or average *hourly* wage income per worker. Which is more important – the total income of wage-earners, or their reward for a given amount of work? (Higher hourly rates need not imply higher average annual income if unemployment rises or more leisure is taken.) To choose, as Myrdal dramatically puts it, one must 'rack one's soul' – less dramatically, one must make a value-judgement. But this causes no problems, unless different investigators, having chosen differently without realizing it, then argue at cross-purposes. Such cross-purposes result from lack of clear definitions rather than lack of a common language.

Measuring changes in *real* wages would require, also, the construction of an *index* to measure changes in the cost of living. 'Cost of living' is also a rather vague, and besides, a *multidimensional* concept – that is, it summarizes many different elements (in this case, consumer prices). In practice, it is impossible to keep track of all such prices; nor are all of equal importance. One has to choose a few 'important' prices, 'weight' them according to their importance, and construct the index as a weighted average. In this way, again, values govern the specification of concepts, and different specifications are possible.

The specification of any vague, multidimensional concept requires similar choices. Take 'racial prejudice'. In one attempt to measure the level of racial prejudice in Britain, the following four questions were put to a sample of British citizens: (1) Would you avoid having coloured neighbours? (2) Are coloured people inferior? (3) Should they be refused municipal housing? (4) Should private landlords reject coloured tenants?[60] The results presented were percentages of respondents who gave each possible number of 'prejudiced' answers, from four to none. Assuming that the replies are an accurate guide to the respondents' attitudes and behaviour, one might still question the omission of other 'important' manifestations of racial prejudice (e.g. in relation to marriage, employment opportunities, etc.). But it would not be easy, indeed not possible, to compile a definitive list of the elements of race prejudice. And should not some elements in such a list be weighted more heavily than others in the construction of any 'prejudice index', as representing more important forms of prejudice? The construction of such an index would, once again, reflect many value-judgements.

Some problems arising from the vague and multidimensional nature of social science concepts are illustrated by the lengthy controversy among sociologists of religion as to whether modern industrial societies are 'secularized'. As Stark and Glock have pointed out[61] in a recent study, much of this controversy has been at cross-purposes between writers adopting different criteria (specifications) of 'secularization' and 'religiousness' – church membership, orthodox belief, etc. Partly these differences reflect different views as to what is important in religion; but in addition writers friendly to religion have tended to specify it in terms that minimize the degree of secularization, while those hostile to religion have done the opposite. (Both groups, perhaps, share a 'democratic' tendency to accept the validity of popular verdicts, or simply a reluctance to admit unwelcome facts.) Where alternative specifications of a concept are possible, such covertly propagandistic specifications are always a danger. The antidote, again, is clear and express definition.

Another long-running controversy, this time in political science, in which evaluative differences confuse an apparently factual argument, is over the 'power élite' thesis – that is, the thesis that certain societies (those with capitalist economies and elective forms of government) are, contrary to their official ideology, ruled by a small élite.[62] This is a thesis about the distribution of *power*. But power is exercised in relation to many different areas of human life, hence to talk of *the* distribution of power implies (apart from any other difficulties involved) some

[60] N. Deakin *et al.*, *Colour, Citizenship and British Society* (London, Panther, 1970), ch. 12.

[61] R. Stark and C. Y. Glock, *Patterns of Religious Commitment*, vol. I (Berkeley, University of California Press, 1970), pp. 11–12.

[62] The best-known protagonists are C. Wright Mills, *The Power Elite* (New York, Oxford U.P., 1956); and R. A. Dahl, 'A Critique of the Ruling Elite Model', *American Political Science Review*, vol. 52 (1958), pp. 463–9, *Who Governs?* (New Haven, Yale U.P., 1961), etc.

'weighting' of these different areas, reflecting their relative importance.[63] This weighting is usually vague and implicit only – hence the cross-purposes. A second source of confusion arises here (as also in the secularization controversy) from the so-called 'only-fully' problem. Those who assert and deny the power élite thesis usually do not specify what minimum *degree* of inequality in the distribution of power it implies; rather (supposing that they have established to their own satisfaction what the distribution of power is) they measure the existing degree of inequality against an unstated standard of what it ought to be. Those who disagree over the power élite thesis may thus not disagree over any matter of fact; but while for one investigator the inequality in the distribution of power is *only* of a given degree, and hence there is no power élite, for another it is *fully* of that degree, and hence a power élite exists. To both, of course, a power élite is a bad thing (they share, in a vague way, the democratic faith), but, because the concept is not clearly specified, the fact that they actually differ as to how much inequality of power is tolerable leads, once again, to cross-purposes.

The morality of social science
The various examples discussed above illustrate how the value-relevance of social science concepts can lead to confusion of fact and value; they do not show that the two cannot be separated, or that a value-free social science, in Weber's sense, is impossible. However, we must now consider an argument against value-free social science which uses a distinction between the physical and social sciences in some respects similar to that involved in Weber's own doctrine of value-relevance.

The argument is that of Jürgen Habermas,[64] a leading theorist of the contemporary 'Frankfurt school'. Habermas notes that the interest of the physical (or 'empirical-analytic') sciences is in empirically corroborated laws—that is, in a way of describing the world which facilitates *technical control* over it. The social sciences ('systematic sciences of social action'), while also seeking 'nomological knowledge' (knowledge of laws), must go on to distinguish those social regularities which are necessary to social life as such from 'relations of dependence' that belong only to particular forms of society, and can be transformed. In so doing, social science initiates the transformation of the latter (Marxist theory, for example, by pointing out that the laws of capitalist society are not eternal but can be abolished by transforming that form of society into a more equal one, can initiate this transformation). This shows, for Habermas, that social science derives from an 'emancipatory

[63] Cf. R. P. Wolff, *The Poverty of Liberalism* (Boston, Beacon paperback, 1969), p. 94.
[64] See J. Habermas, *Knowledge and Human Interests* (London, Heinemann, 1972), pp. 308–17.

interest' in human life, by contrast with the interest in technical control over nature from which physical science springs; in showing that certain social structures impose unnecessary restrictions on human freedom, social science units 'knowledge and interest' – that is, the human interest in freedom, in *responsibility* and *autonomy*. These values, says Habermas, 'possess theoretical certainty'. That members of society should be responsible and autonomous individuals is a scientific value-judgement, for only in such a society is a genuine rational consensus on the truth possible. 'To this extent', says Habermas, 'the truth of statements is based on anticipating the realization of the good life', and 'is linked in the last analysis to the intention of the good and true life'.[65] In social science, it seems, a statement is true only if it promotes the good.

This argument is partly reminiscent of Strauss; partly, too, it extrapolates Popper's account of scientific method, according to which objective consensual knowledge depends crucially on the equal freedom of individuals to pursue that knowledge as members of scientific communities. That, however, does not imply that all men should be free, equal, autonomous or responsible in all areas of life. Even valid scientific knowledge does not require this, for not all men are scientists, nor is science the whole of life even for scientists. Science (including social science) *can* be successfully pursued by a privileged minority in a highly unequal and *otherwise* authoritarian society. And while social science *can* (and perhaps *should*) devote itself to showing how freedom can be realized, it is not the case that (as Strauss also would hold)[66] it *must* do so; if it does, the knowledge will also be useful to those who wish to prevent its realization. Knowledge of how repressive social structures can be changed may thus spring, not from an 'emancipatory interest', but from the very opposite motive – the desire of, say, an authoritarian régime to ward off such changes. Nor is it the case, as Habermas seems to assume, that all social regularities are either necessary to social life, or else repressive and alterable; some may be alterable but not repressive. In a society of autonomous and responsible individuals, would there not be such regularities? For example, the members of such a society might meet regularly to decide freely the conditions of their lives; this regularity could be abolished by establishing a dictatorship. Thus, the insight that certain social regularities are alterable also need not spring from an 'emancipatory interest'. As we have noticed before, we must face the fact that knowledge can always be used to further bad ends. Fact and value are distinct.

Value-relevance and value-freedom

We turn now to arguments which hold that, contrary to Weber, the

---

[65] *Knowledge and Human Interests*, pp. 314, 317.
[66] See above, p. 137.

value-relevance of social science concepts makes value-free social science logically impossible. Such an argument forms part of Leo Strauss's position. Strauss holds an objectivist theory of values; for him, therefore (unlike Weber), value-relevance does not mean relevance to whatever values an investigator may hold, but relevance to an objective scheme of values which determines unequivocally what is significant. Also, whereas for Weber social science concepts must have a value-free *definition* (their value-relevance means only that these definitions pick out phenomena held to be significant by the investigator), Strauss holds that significant social phenomena cannot be defined in a value-free way.[67] Take for example the concept 'art'. In a much-quoted rhetorical question, Strauss asks: 'Would one not laugh out of court a man who claimed to have written a sociology of art but who actually had written a sociology of trash?' There are indeed men who claim to write the sociology of art; Strauss asserts that in categorizing something as 'art' (rather than 'trash') the sociologist must evaluate it – for nothing is art, Strauss implies, unless it achieves a certain aesthetic standard.

Strauss puts forward a similar case in relation to the concept 'religion'. The sociologist of religion must be able to distinguish *genuine* from *spurious* religion. Genuine religion, in Strauss's view, cannot be defined non-evaluatively (in terms of belief in a god or gods, etc.), but involves a morally admirable attitude towards deity. He writes:

'The sociologist of religion cannot help noting the difference between those who try to gain the favour of their gods by flattering or bribing them, and those who try to gain it by a change of heart. . . . Is he not forced to realise that the attempt to bribe the gods is tantamount to trying to be the lord or employer of the gods and that there is a fundamental incongruity between such attempts and what men divine when speaking of gods?'

We saw earlier that the ordinary concept of 'religion' (or 'religiousness') is complex and multidimensional, and that sociologists can easily argue at cross-purposes about it. Strauss, for his part, clearly has no doubts about what genuine religion is. But his argument rests on the claim that genuine religion can be recognized intuitively, although no value-free definition of it can be given. Unfortunately for Strauss, the passage cited goes a long way to undermine that claim. It makes clear that, for Strauss, *attempting to gain the favour of gods by a change of heart* is a genuinely religious phenomenon; *attempting to gain the favour of gods by flattering or bribing them* is not. Why the distinction? Because the latter, unlike the former, involves seeking a position of superiority over the gods ('trying to be [their] lord or employer'). Here, then, is

[67] See *Natural Right and History*, pp. 50–3.

something very like a value-free criterion for distinguishing genuine from spurious religion. What is more, the rationale of this criterion is that seeking a position of superiority over any being is actually incompatible with considering that being to be a god. So it looks as if Strauss does after all want to define religion in terms of belief in gods, i.e. belief in supernatural *and superior* beings. This is a value-free definition, equally applicable by Strauss or by an atheist.

Although Strauss's argument on religion is unconvincing, he may have a better case in relation to 'art'. It is, indeed, perfectly normal to use the term 'art' in a sense which includes an element of favourable evaluation not replaceable by any value-free description. But, contrary to Strauss's belief, art *in this sense* is not a scientifically usable concept. What, then, of the 'sociology of art'? This has to define 'art' in a different, non-evaluative way – possibly as a class of artefacts *treated* as art (in the evaluative sense) by particular sorts of individuals (producers, public, critics, patrons, etc.) whose relations constitute a recognizable social institution. It is always possible that no value-free definition captures the distinctions that seem significant to a particular individual (such as Strauss); but some such definition is necessary before the concept 'art' can feature in scientific propositions. Propositions about 'great art' – such as that all great art is produced by neurotic individuals, or by highly unequal societies – are not scientific propositions.

Strauss's main contention must, then, be rejected. But his argument reminds us that a good many non-scientific concepts (not only 'art') combine evaluative and descriptive elements; when (as often happens) such concepts are transferred to the social sciences, great care is necessary. Take, for example, the concept 'aggression'. This is a phenomenon of great value-relevance because of the fear that human aggressiveness may cause a holocaust – hence there is much interest in its sociological causes and precipitants. But in everyday usage the concept 'aggression' has an evaluative component. Aggression is *unprovoked* attack, or attack on a scale out of proportion to the provocation offered; whether an action constitutes provocation, or sufficient provocation to justify a given attack, is a matter of moral judgement. It seems uncertain whether a useful value-free definition of aggression is possible; if not, sociologists have no alternative but to drop the concept in favour of related but less problematic notions such as conflict, violence, and war.

Another important topic which is problematic in this way is 'crime'. The value-relevance of crime is that it is an evil, to be minimized as much as possible. But 'crime' (like 'art') is an ambiguous term; it may refer to an infringement of a State's criminal law (a value-free definition), or to a seriously immoral or harmful action (a value-laden one). The latter definition is not scientifically usable; but the former too may be unsatisfactory in that the class of actions it picks out may in some cases lack relevance to one's values. Actions forbidden by law normally include trivial offences (such as parking offences) and sometimes include actions which (it could reasonably be held) are in themselves quite blameless (such as miscegenation, the use of cannabis etc.). Criminologists therefore tend to focus on 'serious' crimes, that is, actions contrary to law which they themselves consider serious – in other words a conflation of evaluative and non-evaluative criteria. For example, there is a well-known study by T. C. Willett[68] which sets out to test various hypotheses about 'serious motoring offenders', and concludes, *inter alia*, that they are much more likely than other people to have previous convictions for non-motoring offences. Strictly speaking, the hypotheses and conclusion are not in a scientifically acceptable form. In fact Willett, on the basis partly of existing British legislation and partly of his own value-judgements, included six offences in the category 'serious motoring offence' (causing death by dangerous driving; driving recklessly or dangerously; driving under the influence of drink or drugs; driving while disqualified; failing to insure against third-party risks; failing to stop after, or report, an accident). His findings, properly speaking, relate to these six classes of offenders; whether they coincide with the category 'serious motoring offenders' is a matter of opinion.

Let us turn now to another argument from the value-relevance of social science concepts to the logical impossibility of value-free social science – that of the distinguished economist and sociologist, Gunnar Myrdal. Myrdal in fact discusses two kinds of value-relevant concept. Firstly, there are concepts like 'folkways' and 'mores', introduced by the American sociologist W. G. Sumner. While not in themselves evaluative (they are roughly synonymous with 'customs'), they reflect Sumner's interest in non-governmental determinants of behaviour – an interest which sprang from his hostility to state 'interference' in social life.[69] Secondly, there are concepts like 'equilibrium' and 'economic integration', which, according to Myrdal, are themselves evaluative; that is, they are used not only to describe certain states of affairs but also to imply that they are desirable. For Weber, the first sort of concept in itself gives no ground for criticism, while the second (if Myrdal has characterized it correctly) can find no place in social science. But this is not at all Myrdal's view. Sumner is severely criticized on the grounds that his concepts 'folkways' and 'mores' imply a misleading theory. The theory, apparently, is that folkways and mores are more

---

[68] *Criminal on the Road* (London, Tavistock Publications, 1959). See pp. 43 ff., 78, 130–1, 299 ff. My comments on this book are intended to illustrate my argument rather than as a serious criticism of Willett.

[69] G. Myrdal, *Value in Social Theory*, pp. 78–9, 139–40, 146–9.

powerful than 'stateways' (i.e. government action) – so government action is pointless. Sumner certainly asserted this, no doubt wrongly, and no doubt because of his laissez-faire political views; nevertheless, it is in no way implied by the use of the concepts 'folkways' and 'mores'. It is not part of their *definition* that they are more powerful than 'stateways'. The concepts themselves are subject to criticism only if they have no application to anything of significance, and that is not the case.

As for 'equilibrium' and 'economic integration', Myrdal charges that these concepts too reflect a laissez-faire philosophy and a hostility to government action.[70] He has in mind the use of these terms in orthodox economics to describe situations supposedly brought about by unrestricted market forces, namely equality of supply and demand for each commodity ('equilibrium') and uniformity of price of each commodity ('integration'). This says Myrdal is to commend these situations, and therefore the free market, in a way which appears scientific but is not and cannot be. But Myrdal does not, like Weber, call for the elimination of such terms; their use is, he holds, the inevitable result of the value-relevance (in Weber's language) of social science concepts:[71] 'The value connotation of our main terms represents our interest in a matter, gives direction to our thoughts and significance to our inferences. It poses the questions without which there are no answers.' It would be in vain, therefore, to try to give terms like 'equilibrium' and 'integration' a purely descriptive 'technical' definition, or to try to replace them by other terms that have the same descriptive meanings but lack their value-connotations; the new terms would quickly come to have the same value-connotations as the old.

Myrdal's solution to the problem, therefore, is that the value-premises that guide research and are reflected in the value-connotations of sociological concepts should be made *explicit*. Then, 'the stated value premises, together with the data (established by theoretical analysis with the use of the same value premises) should [be] the premises for all policy conclusions'.[72] The chosen value-premises should also be 'relevant' and 'significant', that is, should be those held by major social groups.[73] This strategy is exemplified, Myrdal believes, by his own research into race relations in the USA. To guide the research he explicitly looked to the 'American Creed' (the social ethic generally accepted by Americans), in particular its principle of equal opportunity for all. This gave him as the focus of his research the concept of

[70] G. Myrdal, *Value in Social Theory*, pp. 1–4, 138–9.

[71] *Ibid.*, pp. 1–2, 51, 54, 153–5, 163–4, 253.

[72] *Objectivity in Social Research*, p. 55. See also *Value in Social Theory*, pp. 2, 50, 52, 132 and *passim*.

[73] *Value in Social Theory*, pp. 134, 157, 161–4.

'discrimination' (i.e. unequal opportunity), with its negative value-connotations; that is, he sought to discover the extent, causes, etc. of discrimination against the American Negro. Finally, his policy conclusions were guided by the goal of abolishing discrimination and the factual knowledge about it gained through the research. Myrdal claims that by making his value-premise explicit he avoided *bias* but not *one-sidedness*; ideally not just one but all 'relevant and significant' value-premises should guide a series of investigations of the topic in question.

While there is nothing wrong with Myrdal's strategy for investigating American race relations, his general account of fact and value in social science is, in my opinion, riddled with errors. Firstly, why should the researcher's concepts be determined by the values of major social groups? He should, surely, be guided by his own honest judgements of what is important. Nor will he avoid bias by making his value-judgements explicit; he will do so if and only if his value-judgements do not influence his factual assertions. Myrdal is also mistaken in supposing that disagreement about values necessarily implies a difference in the organizing concepts of research. If race relations were investigated by a sociologist who believed that the proper function of Negroes was to serve white men, the same range facts would be of interest to him as to Myrdal, though he would of course evaluate them very differently, and draw very different policy conclusions. Contrary to Myrdal, the value-judgements necessary to draw policy conclusions are quite different from those needed to define research concepts; the former must be judgements that certain states of affairs are *good* and others *bad*, the latter need only be judgements that the existence or non-existence of some state of affairs is *significant*. This latter value-judgement is entailed by *either* of the *opposed* value-judgements, that that state of affairs is good *or* that it is bad. However, Myrdal's doctrine implies that investigators interested in the same phenomenon who disagree as to whether it is good or bad cannot agree on a value-free description of it. This simply is not so. Do those who wield power in the USA (or in Britain) by and large treat Negroes less favourably than white people? Does the free market equate supply and demand, and bring about a uniform price for each commodity? These are all questions of fact, not of value. It scarcely matters whether these postulated states of affairs are labelled 'racial discrimination', 'economic equilibrium' or 'economic integration', so long as it is made clear – as can easily be done – that, if they are, the labels refer only to these factual situations, which it is in principle possible to evaluate either favourably or unfavourably. Alternatively one can (at the price of some clumsiness of expression) eschew the labels, and describe the phenomena in the terms used in the questions above.

Ideology and social science

Before closing this chapter we must consider the work of one further theorist who has attacked the value-freedom doctrine on the basis of the value-relevance of social science concepts – Karl Mannheim. Social science, Mannheim holds, is impossible without 'ethical presuppositions'; without them the social scientist 'has no questions to raise and is not even able to formulate a tentative hypothesis which enables him to set a problem'; for this reason, social science concepts are 'replete with evaluations'.[74] Mannheim's argument here is essentially the same as Myrdal's and does not require separate consideration.

But Mannheim emphasizes much more than Myrdal the role of membership of specific social groups, especially classes, in determining the ethical and ontological presuppositions which mould the individual's descriptions of social reality. Here Mannheim is employing, though in an idiosyncratic way, the Marxist concept of 'ideology'. We shall return to the use Mannheim himself makes of this idea; but first the Marxist conception itself calls for discussion.

Marx held that all societies in which the means of production are privately owned are divided into antagonistic social classes, one of which is the dominant or ruling class. Class conflict culminates in revolution, that is, the overthrow and replacement of the ruling class by a revolutionary class. Ruling and revolutionary classes fortify themselves with appropriate belief systems, which are usually *ideological* – that is, they correspond to the interests of the class in question, and they are at least partly false. A class ideology will include both evaluative beliefs about society (social and political philosophy, etc.), and factual assertions as to how society actually works. Marx's own social theory contains both these elements, and like an ideology is assigned by Marx the historical role of fortifying a revolutionary class (the proletariat) and thus of helping to establish the kind of society it favours. But Marx, naturally, considered his own theory to be true, and in this sense not ideological.

The relevance of this to the value-freedom issue is that it appears to imply that only those who make a particular value-judgement (that is, those who favour communism) can transcend ideology and arrive at true descriptions of social reality. If this were so, the injunction to social scientists not to allow their value-commitments to bias their perception of the facts would be pointless; those who, for example, because of their identification with the bourgeois class and its interests, prefer capitalism to communism, cannot help misdescribing social facts. A man's social science depends on which side he takes in the class struggle.

Yet this is not necessarily the implication of the Marxist theory of

[74] K. Mannheim, *Ideology and Utopia* (London, Routledge and Kegan Paul paperback, 1960), pp. 41–2, 78–9.

ideology. For while it certainly asserts that value-judgements and judgements of fact are intimately linked, it need not be interpreted as claiming that the former determine the latter, rather than vice-versa. It would in fact be reasonable here to make a distinction between social theorists and other individuals. Marx could hold, for example, that an ordinary bourgeois fails to see capitalism as it really is because he is blinkered by his attachment to capitalism as the system favourable to his class interests; on the other hand a social theorist, not himself a bourgeois, might favour capitalism because he had (in the Marxist view) failed to understand its real nature. Correspondingly one who, like Marx, did understand its real nature, would for that reason espouse communism (certainly the value-commitments of Marx and many other Marxist social theorists cannot be accounted for in terms of their class). If, then, a social theorist can *choose* his political position on the basis of how he reads the facts of social life, that reading can be value-free in Weber's sense. Admittedly, the Marxist doctrine implies that in capitalist society there will always be theoretical apologists of capitalism who proffer deluded or dishonest descriptions of how that system works. But it is no part of the value-freedom doctrine to deny the existence of delusion or dishonesty; it denies only that delusions in matters of fact necessarily follow from particular value-commitments.

In addition, the Marxist theory need not be interpreted in a completely deterministic way; that is, even if it asserts that, by and large, theoretical opponents of communism misdescribe social facts because they oppose communism (and not vice-versa), it may still admit the possibility of exceptions. In that case, it allows that an individual anti-communist social scientist is not necessarily incapable of seeing and reporting social truth; so that knowledge of social fact does not absolutely depend on a particular value-commitment.

Political economy

Regardless of the correct interpretation of these points, Marxist theory certainly seems to imply that the great bulk of non-Marxist 'social science' is nothing more than ideology whose function is to further the interests of the bourgeoisie.[75] There is no space here for an adequate appraisal of this grave charge, but it is worth looking at one discipline which perhaps more than any other has been its target – orthodox economics. It should be borne in mind that, to qualify as ideology, an assertion need not be *totally* false. The Marxist term 'reification', in one of its senses, refers to a mistaken belief that the laws of society are as fixed and absolute as physical laws of nature. Many economic laws, for example, apply only to a capitalist market system, even to particular

[75] This charge is made explicitly by M. Nicolaus, *op. cit.*, pp. 45–60.

phases only of its evolution. Things that are impossible under one economic system are therefore not necessarily absolutely impossible. Failure to realize this can justifiably be described as an ideological illusion.

Marx himself considered many of the so-called classical economists to be 'sophists and sycophants' of the ruling class.[76] The greatest of them, Smith and Ricardo, he admired up to a point, but still felt that they were to some extent victims of illusion. Yet it is hard indeed to see Smith, at any rate, as in any sense an ideologist of the bourgeoisie. A major theme of his *Wealth of Nations* is the divergence between the public interest, and the interest of merchants and manufacturers in excluding competition so as to increase their profit.[77] They thus, says Smith 'levy, for their own benefit, an absurd tax on the rest of their fellow-citizens'. Any proposal of theirs 'ought always to be listened to . . . with the most suspicious attention', for they 'have generally an interest to deceive the public and . . . accordingly have, upon many occasions, deceived and oppressed it'. It is precisely in order to counter the 'monopolizing spirit of merchants and manufacturers'[78] that Smith so vigorously advocates free trade. His hostility to monopolies became part of the consensus of classical 'political economy'.

Nevertheless, it is not hard to find ideological assertions in the work of classical economists.[79] Senior, for example, who played a large part in drafting the harsh Poor Law of 1834, believed (quite falsely) that in the existing economic situation an able-bodied man could, if he chose, always find work and earn a living by it, but would be unlikely to do so unless the alternative was poverty. It was thus natural to see harsh treatment of the indigent as both merited by their indolence and necessary to national prosperity. Senior also believed that any reduction in the inordinately long hours worked in textile mills would make the industry unprofitable and, again, harm national prosperity. Almost all the classical economists agreed that wage levels could increase in the long term only if the labouring class restricted procreation and hence the supply of labourers; many, indeed, held that this almost certainly could not happen – any increase in wages would rapidly lead to a corresponding increase in the labouring population, which would bring wages down again.

It is not hard to see how such beliefs, now discredited, might be

[76] Quoted in M. M. Bober, *Karl Marx's Interpretation of History*, 2nd edn (New York, Norton, 1965), p. 161. See also pp. 162–3.

[77] *The Wealth of Nations*, ed. E. Cannan (London, Methuen, 1961), vol. 1, pp. 277–8.

[78] *Ibid.*, p. 519.

[79] The examples quoted are taken from A. W. Coats (ed.), *The Classical Economists and Economic Policy* (London, Methuen, 1971), pp. 83, 111, 156–7, 163–70.

congenial to the employing class. The important point, however, is that they *are* now discredited. A social science can correct its own mistakes, including ideological mistakes. To see the mistakes made by the classical economists, it has not been necessary for economists in general to become communists. Perhaps it has been necessary for them to *listen* to communists, but that is quite a different matter. Marxists, undoubtedly, would claim that orthodox economics is nevertheless still a capitalist ideology, and this is the sort of charge that cannot be comprehensively refuted – one can consider specific charges only. Obviously not all possible examples of alleged ideology can be discussed here, but it will be worthwhile to look at one such allegation which is both representative and important.

In a recent article Edward Nell[80] charges that orthodox economic theory falsely represents income under capitalism as received in *exchange* for contributions to production – wages and salaries in return for labour services, dividends and other forms of profit income in return for the supply of capital. In fact, says Nell, profit income is not received in exchange for anything – owners of capital make no contribution to production. Nell's point clearly is that owners of capital do not *deserve* to derive any income from their ownership (the entire product should go to labour), and that orthodox economic theory suggests otherwise. But the latter assertion is mistaken. There is no doubt that private owners of capital control the supply of a factor of production, and make it available in return for an income. It is in this sense only that economic theory represents profit income as the result of an exchange. Whether those who control capital funds *ought* to have this control, whether they should be able to obtain income because of it – these are evaluative questions which economic theory does not and cannot answer. The orthodox theory of income distribution is perfectly compatible with Nell's Marxist value-commitments.

Our discussion of ideology and economics, though inevitably very incomplete, suffices to show, I hope, that the espousing of a particular value-position need never dictate one's reading of the facts and that there is no compelling reason why social scientists with fundamentally different value-commitments need read social facts in incompatible ways. Opposite evaluations of capitalism have in fact been combined with similar factual judgements about it. Marx himself, who hated capitalism, predicted its overthrow and replacement by socialism; but so did one of the most vigorous champions of the capitalist system, Joseph Schumpeter.[81]

[80] 'Economics: the Revival of Political Economy', in R. Blackburn (ed.), *op. cit.*, pp. 86–92.

[81] See his *Capitalism, Socialism, and Democracy*, 4th edn (London, Allen and Unwin, 1954), Part II.

From ideology to the relativity of truth

So far we have not questioned the assumption of Marxists that, whoever else may be guilty of ideological thinking, they are not. It is, however, extremely tempting to do so. Why, one might ask, should the proletariat be a privileged class, such that identification with its interests alone provides the key to a true sociological vision? May it not be the case that commitment to the cause of any social group is an obstacle to objectivity? With this question we return to Karl Mannheim; for Mannheim's theory starts from the proposition that everyone belongs to some social group, which has its characteristic interests and values, and these enter into the individual's perception of the social world.[82]

Despite its considerable renown, Mannheim's theory is not easy to expound. One reason for this is suggested by what Mannheim himself says of his own exposition: 'Contradictions have not been corrected because . . . a given theoretical sketch may often have latent in it varied possibilities which must be permitted to come to expression in order that the scope of the exposition may be fully appreciated'.[83] This frank admission of self-contradiction has a certain charm, but one is somewhat nonplussed when a distinguished intellectual sees no need to make his theory coherent.

What, then, are some of the 'possibilities' to which Mannheim gives 'expression'? As we have seen, he stresses the dependence of sociological conceptualization on social position and its concomitant evaluations; and for him, this 'value-relevance' of concepts implies bias and lack of scientific objectivity in the *statements* that employ these concepts[84] (Weber is criticized for his 'assumption of the separability of theory and evaluation').[85] Sometimes the 'bias' involved seems to be merely the fact that any set of social concepts represents only one of several possible ways of describing a social situation – ways which need not *contradict* one another, though each will be in a sense limited and partial. On the whole, though, it seems that this is not Mannheim's meaning; his concern, he says, is with 'divergent and conflicting',[86] not merely limited, viewpoints. Mannheim, in fact, conflates the Weberian theme of value-relevance and the Marxian theme of ideology.

Can this bias in assertions about social phenomena be overcome? Mannheim's answer is complicated. Like Myrdal, he recommends that the evaluative presuppositions lying behind factual judgements should be raised to consciousness and made explicit. But (again as for Myrdal) this is not sufficient to overcome one-sidedness; there must therefore also be a *synthesis* of the various different viewpoints into 'the most comprehensive view of the world which is attainable at a given time'.[87]

---

[82] *Ideology and Utopia*, pp. 26, 51 and *passim*.   [83] *Ibid.*, p. 47.
[84] *Ibid.*, pp. 4–5, 36, 42–3, 70–2, 86–7, and *passim*.   [85] *Ibid.*, p. 145n.
[86] *Ibid.*, p. 91.   [87] *Ibid.*, p. 135. See also pp. 91–2, 146, 270–1.

The group best placed to achieve such a synthesis is, for Mannheim, the intelligentsia (we might say, the social scientists), because it is socially relatively detached ('*freischwebend*' or free-floating); its members are of very heterogeneous class origin yet share a common educational heritage – hence the intelligentsia as a group is in a position to achieve a consensus which as it were pools the viewpoints of other social strata.[88]

The exalted role accorded by Mannheim to the intelligentsia (his own social group) has aroused much scorn, for example from Popper.[89] Yet this part of Mannheim's theory is by no means ridiculous – his conception of the intelligentsia, in fact, is not so very different from Popper's own picture of the scientific community.[90] (Admittedly Popper stresses the latter's attachment to the norms of scientific method rather than its social position and composition. But the latter are not irrelevant.) Much more dubious, however, is Mannheim's idea of a synthesis of conflicting assertions. For Mannheim, it appears, this would be achieved through the 'sociology of knowledge', a discipline which has the task of explaining why each group holds the view of social reality that it does.[91] In principle, to *explain* why conflicting assertions are made is not to *synthesize* them; even when explained, any and all of the assertions could be rejected as completely false. But in Mannheim's view there is an important distinction between mere error, and the unavoidable one-sidedness of a social group's viewpoint. In so far as the sociology of knowledge shows that the latter applies to some belief of a group, it shows (Mannheim holds) that *the belief is correct from the point of view of that group*. Thus, if two groups (x and y) hold conflicting beliefs, they can be synthesized (and the conflict removed) by the formula that, from the point of view of group x, x's belief is correct, while from the point of view of group y, y's belief is correct. As Mannheim puts it: 'It lies in the nature of certain assertions that they cannot be formulated absolutely, but only in terms of the perspective of a given situation'.[92]

Which assertions, exactly? What about the synthetic social science achievable by the free-floating intelligentsia, with its explanations of why particular views are held by particular groups, its demonstrations that they could not but hold the views they hold, etc. (we need not worry about what else it might contain)? Can *these* assertions lay claim to an absolutely objective status? Mannheim's answer is negative.[93] The free-floating intelligentsia can, after all, achieve only relative, and

---

[88] *Ideology and Utopia*, pp. 136–43.
[89] *The Open Society and its Enemies*, vol. 2, pp. 213–16.
[90] See above, p. 146.
[91] *Ideology and Utopia*, pp. 42, 71–2, 226–7, 238, 253–5, 270–1.
[92] *Ibid.*, p. 254.   [93] *Ibid.*, pp. 43, 70–1, 89n., 135, 274.

not absolute, detachment – its synthesis, therefore, is only the best (because the most comprehensive) possible at the time, it has to be continually reformulated and never achieves a definitive form. In relation to social life and history, therefore, 'it is impossible to conceive of absolute truth existing independently of the values and [social] position of the subject'. In brief, there are no value-free social facts.

It is instructive to compare Mannheim's philosophy of social science with Popper's philosophy of science in general.[94] The two share the view that the scientific consensus of any given moment is not the last word – it may always need revision in the light of further experience. For Mannheim, however, the scientific consensus is itself the only possible standard of truth – hence the consensus of a particular time is always true in a relative sense, but there is no description of social reality that is true in a non-relative sense; whereas for Popper social reality is an objective fact, a description of it is true if and only if it corresponds to the reality, and the scientific consensus, at any moment, may in principle be true or false (though, given human fallibility, it is unlikely to be completely true).

This contrast, I believe, makes clear Mannheim's fundamental mistake, namely, his view that if the limitations of a belief spring from the limitations of the social or historical viewpoint of those who hold it, that belief cannot be described as simply false, but only as false in a relative sense, and is therefore also true in a relative sense. But it is simply a mistake to think that if error is inevitable it is therefore only relative. If two beliefs – either of different social groups, or of the synthesizing intelligentsia at different periods – genuinely 'conflict', one at least must be false in the ordinary sense. We can thus reject Mannheim's picture of an endless series of conflicting relative truths, each indissolubly connected with a different set of value-commitments; rather, in so far as value-commitments associated with some social or historical position influence judgements of social fact, they are more likely to lead to errors. Yet another attempt to rebut the value-freedom doctrine seems to have failed. I know of none that succeeds.

[94] See above, pp. 13–19.

BIBLIOGRAPHY

A *Books and Articles*

BLALOCK, H. M. Jr., *Social Statistics* (New York, McGraw-Hill, 1960).

BRAITHWAITE, R. B., *Scientific Explanation* (Cambridge U.P., 1953).

BROWN, R., *Explanation in Social Science* (London, Routledge and Kegan Paul, 1963).

COHEN, P. S., *Modern Social Theory* (London, Heinemann, 1968).

DAVIS, K., 'The Myth of Functional Analysis as a Special Method in Sociology and Anthropology', *American Sociological Review*, vol. 24 (1959).

DONAGAN, A., 'Alternative Historical Explanations and their Verification', *The Monist*, vol. 53 (1969).

DORE, R. P., 'Function and Cause', *American Sociological Review*, vol. 26 (1961).

DRAY, W. H., *Laws and Explanation in History* (London, Oxford U.P., 1957).

DRAY, W. H., 'Singular Hypotheticals and Historical Explanation', in L. Gross (ed.), *Sociological Theory* (London, Harper and Row, 1967).

DRAY, W. H., 'The Historical Explanation of Action Reconsidered', in S. Hook (ed.), *Philosophy and History* (New York U.P., 1963).

DURKHEIM, E., *The Rules of Sociological Method* (Glencoe, Free Press paperback, 1964).

GARDINER, P., *The Nature of Historical Explanation* (London, Oxford U.P., paperback, 1968).

GIBSON, Q., *The Logic of Social Enquiry* (London, Routledge and Kegan Paul, 1960).

GOULDNER, A. W., 'Anti-Minotaur: The Myth of a Value-Free Sociology', in I. L. Horowitz (ed.), *The New Sociology* (New York, Oxford U.P., 1964).

HABERMAS, J., *Knowledge and Human Interests* (London, Heinemann, 1972).

HARRÉ, R., *Principles of Scientific Thinking* (London, MacMillan, 1970).

HAYEK, F. A., *The Counter-Revolution of Science* (Glencoe, Free Press paperback, 1964).

HEMPEL, C. G., *Aspects of Scientific Explanation* (New York, Free Press, 1965).

HEMPEL, C. G., *Philosophy of Natural Science* (Englewood Cliffs, Prentice-Hall, 1966).

HEMPEL, C. G., 'Rational Action', *Proceedings and Addresses of the American Philosophical Association*, vol. XXV, 1962.

HOMANS, G. C., *Sentiments and Activities* (London, Routledge and Kegan Paul, 1962).

HOMANS, G. C., *The Nature of Social Science* (New York, Harcourt, Brace and World, 1967).

HUME, D., *A Treatise of Human Nature* (many editions).

ISAJIW, W. W., *Causation and Functionalism in Sociology* (London, Routledge and Kegan Paul, 1968).

JONES, R. E., *The Functional Analysis of Politics* (London, Routledge and Kegan Paul, 1967).

KUHN, T. S., *The Structure of Scientific Revolutions* (Chicago U.P., 1962).

LESSNOFF, M. H., 'Functionalism and Explanation in Social Science', *Sociological Review*, new series, vol. 17 (1969).

LITTLE, I. D. M., *A Critique of Welfare Economics* (London, Oxford U.P., 1950).

MACINTYRE, A., *Against the Self-Images of the Age* (London, Duckworth, 1971).

MACKIE, J. L., 'Causes and Conditions', *American Philosophical Quarterly*, vol. 2 (1965).

MALINOWSKI, B., *A Scientific Theory of Culture* (New York, Oxford U.P., 1960).

MANNHEIM, K., *Ideology and Utopia* (London, Routledge and Kegan Paul paperback, 1960).

MARCUSE, H., *Negations* (London, Allen Lane, 1968).

MELDEN, A. I., *Free Action* (London, Routledge and Kegan Paul, 1961).

MERTON, R., *On Theoretical Sociology* (New York, Free Press, 1967).

MILL, J. S., *System of Logic* (many editions).

MISHAN, E. J., 'A Survey of Welfare Economics, 1939–59', *Economic Journal*, vol. 70 (1960).

MYRDAL, G., *Objectivity in Social Research* (London, Duckworth, 1970).

MYRDAL, G., *Value in Social Theory* (London, Routledge and Kegan Paul, 1958), with Introduction by P. Streeten.

NAGEL, E., *The Structure of Science* (London, Routledge and Kegan Paul, 1961).

NEEDHAM, R., *Structure and Sentiment* (Chicago U.P., 1962).

PAP, A., *Introduction to the Philosophy of Science* (Glencoe, Free Press, 1962).

POPPER, K. R., *The Logic of Scientific Discovery*, revised edn (London, Hutchinson, 1968).

POPPER, K. R., *The Open Society and its Enemies* (London, Routledge and Kegan Paul paperback, 1962), vol. 2.

POPPER, K. R., *The Poverty of Historicism* (London, Routledge and Kegan Paul paperback, 1961).

RADCLIFFE-BROWN, A. R., *Structure and Function in Primitive Society* (London, Cohen and West, 1952).

REX, J., *Key Problems of Sociological Theory* (London, Routledge and Kegan Paul paperback, 1970).

RICKMAN, H. P., *Understanding and the Human Studies* (London, Heinemann, 1967).

ROBBINS, L., *The Nature and Significance of Economic Science*, 2nd edn (London, Macmillan, 1948).

ROSENBLUETH, A., and WIENER, N., 'Purposeful and Non-Purposeful Behaviour', *Philosophy of Science*, vol. 17 (1950).

ROSENBLUETH, A., WIENER, N., and BIGELOW, J., 'Behaviour, Purpose, and Teleology', *Philosophy of Science*, vol. X (1943).

RUNCIMAN, W. G., *Sociology in its Place* (Cambridge U.P., 1970).

RYAN, A., *The Philosophy of the Social Sciences* (London, Macmillan, 1970).

SCHEFFLER, I., *Science and Subjectivity* (Indianapolis, Bobbs-Merrill, 1967).

SCHUTZ, A., *Phenomenology of the Social World* (Evanston, Northwestern U.P., 1967).

SIEGEL, S., *Non-Parametric Statistics for the Behavioural Sciences* (New York, McGraw-Hill, 1956).

SKINNER, B. F., *Beyond Freedom and Dignity* (London, Cape, 1972).

SPIRO, M. E., 'Causes, Functions, and Cross-Cousin Marriage', *Journal of the Royal Anthropological Institute of Great Britain and Ireland*, vol. 94 (1964).

STRAUSS, L., *Natural Right and History* (Chicago U.P., 1953).

STRAUSS, L., *What is Political Philosophy?* (New York, Free Press, 1959).

TAYLOR, C., *The Explanation of Behaviour* (London, Routledge and Kegan Paul, 1964).

TAYLOR, R., 'Rejoinder' to Rosenblueth and Wiener, *Philosophy of Science*, vol. 17 (1950).

TAYLOR, R., 'Thought and Purpose', *Inquiry*, vol. 12 (1969).

VON WRIGHT, G. H., *Explanation and Understanding* (London, Routledge and Kegan Paul, 1971).

WADDINGTON, C. H., *The Ethical Animal* (London, Allen and Unwin, 1960).

WEBER, M., *The Methodology of the Social Sciences* (Glencoe, Free Press, 1949).

WEBER, M., *The Theory of Social and Economic Organization* (Glencoe, Free Press paperback, 1964), with Introduction by T. Parsons.

WINCH, P., *The Idea of a Social Science,* (London, Routledge and Kegan Paul, 1958).

B *Useful Anthologies* (almost all of which contain pieces mentioned in the body of this book).

BLACKBURN, R. (ed.), *Ideology in Social Science* (London, Fontana, 1972).

BORGER, R., and CIOFFI, F. (eds), *Explanation in the Behavioral Sciences* (Cambridge U.P., 1970).

BRODBECK, M. (ed.), *Readings in the Philosophy of the Social Sciences* (New York, Macmillan, 1968).

BRODY, B. (ed.), *Readings in the Philosophy of Science* (Englewood Cliffs, Prentice-Hall, 1970).

DRAY, W. H. (ed.), *Philosophical Analysis and History* (New York, Harper and Row, 1966).

EMMET, D., and MACINTYRE, A. (eds), *Sociological Theory and Philosophical Analysis* (London, Macmillan, 1970).

KRIMERMAN, L. I. (ed.), *The Nature and Scope of Social Science* (New York, Appleton-Century-Crofts, 1969).

LAKATOS, I., and MUSGRAVE, A. (eds), *Criticism and the Growth of Knowledge* (Cambridge U.P., 1970).

LASLETT, P., and RUNCIMAN, W. G. (eds), *Philosophy, Politics and Society, Third Series* (Oxford, Blackwell, 1967).

MORRISON, D. E., and HENKEL, R. E. (eds), *The Significance Test Controversy* (London, Butterworth, 1970).

NATANSON, M. (ed.), *Philosophy of the Social Sciences* (New York, Random House, 1963).

O'NEILL, J. (ed.), *Modes of Individualism and Collectivism* (London, Heinemann, 1973).

RYAN, A. (ed.), *The Philosophy of Social Explanation* (London, Oxford U.P., 1973).

WILSON, B. R. (ed.), *Rationality* (Oxford, Blackwell, 1970).

NAME INDEX

SUBJECT INDEX